THE MOST BRILLIANT
BOLDLY GOING BOOK OF
EXPLORATION EVER
by the Brainwaves

Illustrated by Lisa Swerling and Ralph Lazar

Written by Peter Chrisp

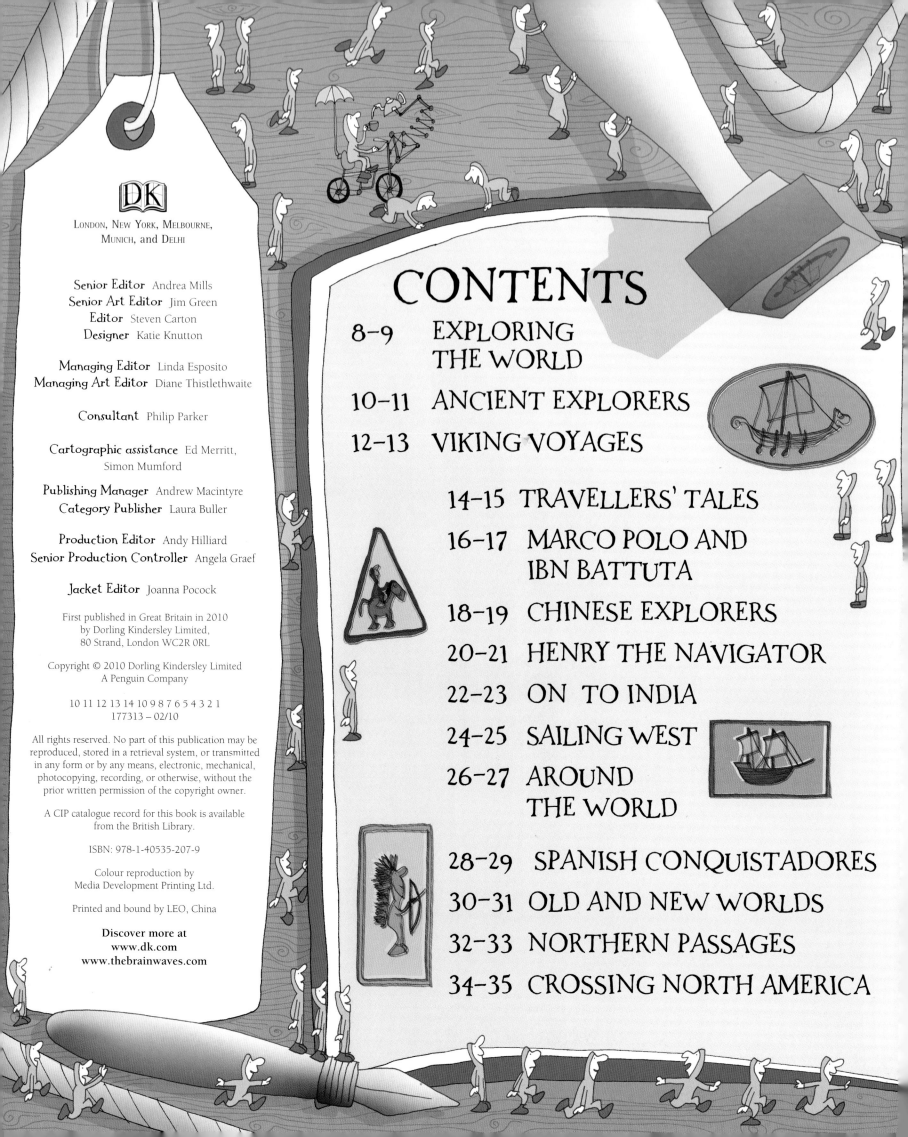

DK

LONDON, NEW YORK, MELBOURNE,
MUNICH, and DELHI

Senior Editor Andrea Mills
Senior Art Editor Jim Green
Editor Steven Carton
Designer Katie Knutton

Managing Editor Linda Esposito
Managing Art Editor Diane Thistlethwaite

Consultant Philip Parker

Cartographic assistance Ed Merritt,
Simon Mumford

Publishing Manager Andrew Macintyre
Category Publisher Laura Buller

Production Editor Andy Hilliard
Senior Production Controller Angela Graef

Jacket Editor Joanna Pocock

First published in Great Britain in 2010
by Dorling Kindersley Limited,
80 Strand, London WC2R 0RL

CONTENTS

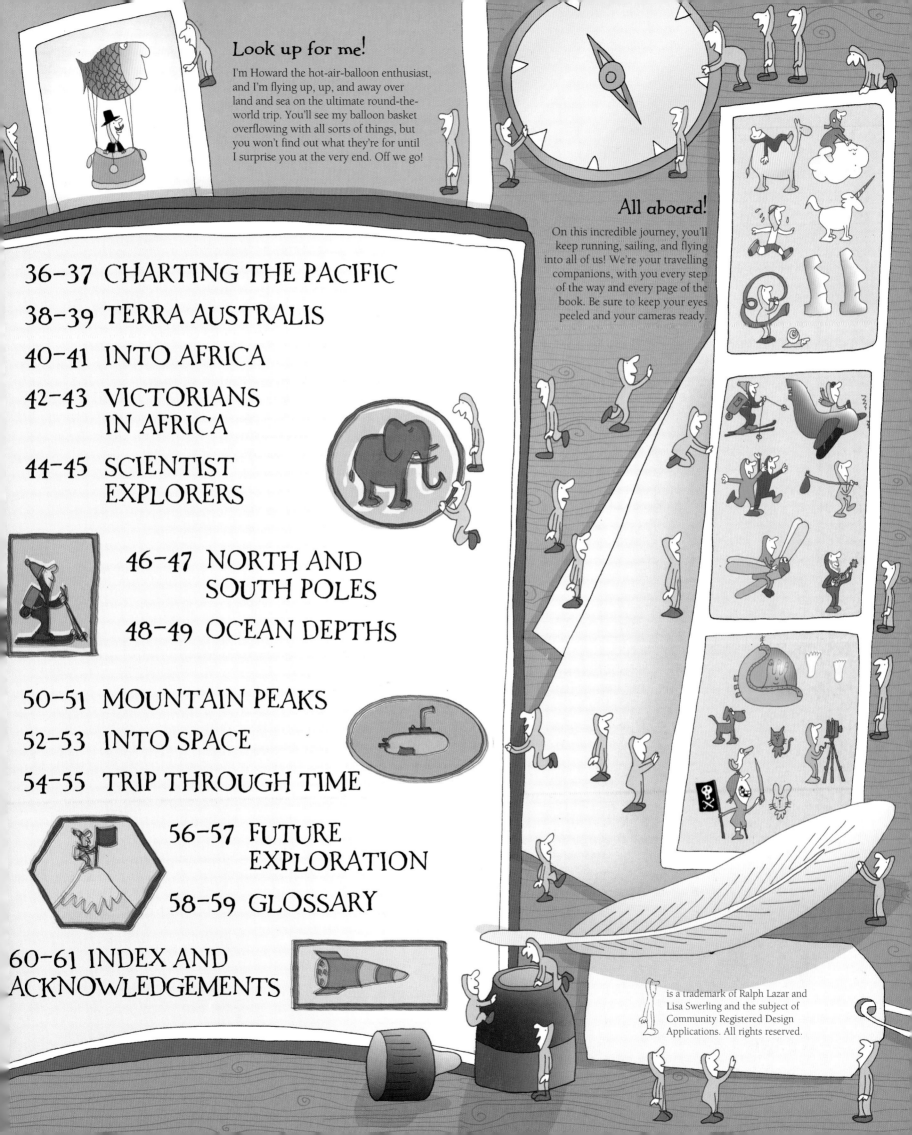

Look up for me!

I'm Howard the hot-air-balloon enthusiast, and I'm flying up, up, and away over land and sea on the ultimate round-the-world trip. You'll see my balloon basket overflowing with all sorts of things, but you won't find out what they're for until I surprise you at the very end. Off we go!

All aboard!

On this incredible journey, you'll keep running, sailing, and flying into all of us! We're your travelling companions, with you every step of the way and every page of the book. Be sure to keep your eyes peeled and your cameras ready.

Exploring the world

As long as there have been people, there have been explorers. In prehistoric times, people managed to settle almost every inhabitable part of the planet. Yet, for most of our history, the human race was divided into many regions, with people in one part of the world unaware of distant lands. It is only in the last few thousands years that explorers have recorded their discoveries. Thanks to their writings and maps, an accurate picture of the world was created.

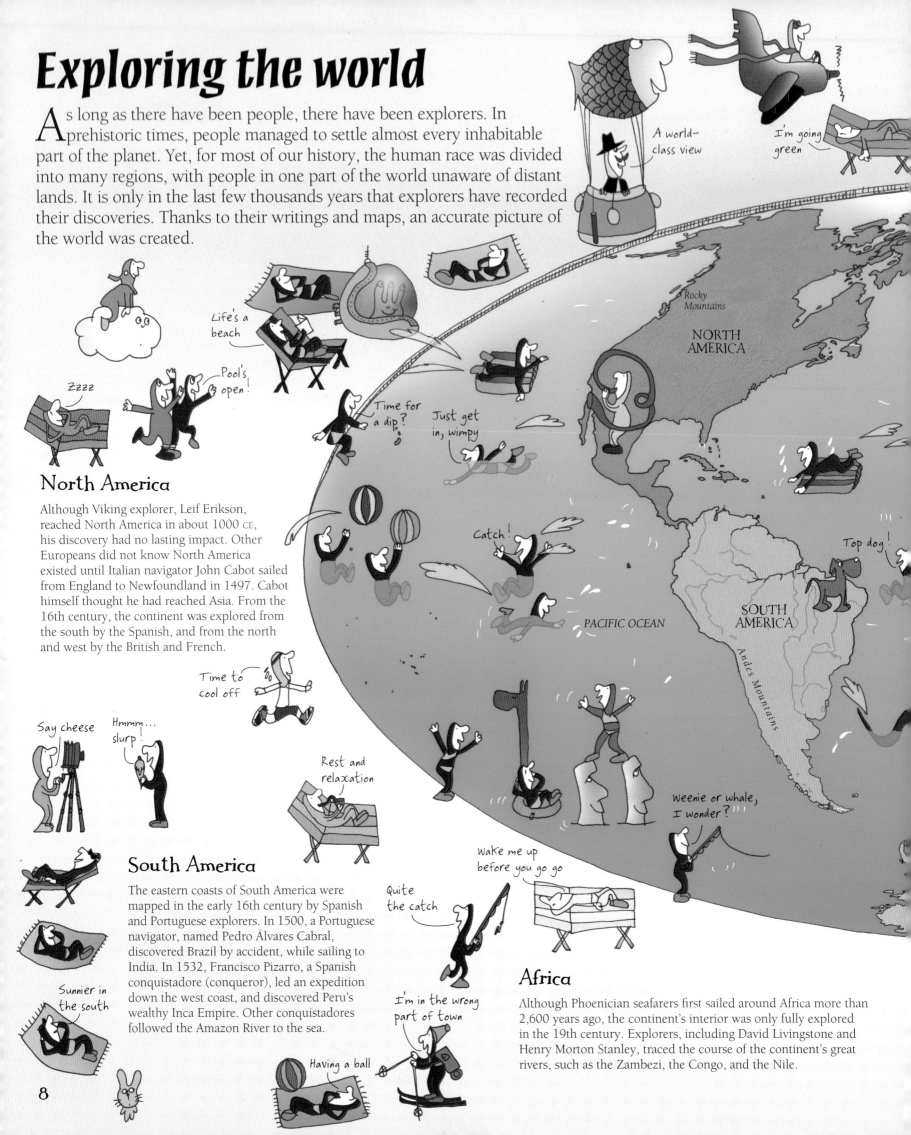

A world-class view

I'm going green

Zzzz

Life's a beach

Pool's open!

Time for a dip?

Just get in, wimpy

Catch!

Rocky Mountains

NORTH AMERICA

Top dog!

SOUTH AMERICA

PACIFIC OCEAN

Andes Mountains

North America

Although Viking explorer, Leif Erikson, reached North America in about 1000 CE, his discovery had no lasting impact. Other Europeans did not know North America existed until Italian navigator John Cabot sailed from England to Newfoundland in 1497. Cabot himself thought he had reached Asia. From the 16th century, the continent was explored from the south by the Spanish, and from the north and west by the British and French.

Time to cool off

Say cheese

Hmmm… slurp!

Rest and relaxation

South America

The eastern coasts of South America were mapped in the early 16th century by Spanish and Portuguese explorers. In 1500, a Portuguese navigator, named Pedro Álvares Cabral, discovered Brazil by accident, while sailing to India. In 1532, Francisco Pizarro, a Spanish conquistadore (conqueror), led an expedition down the west coast, and discovered Peru's wealthy Inca Empire. Other conquistadores followed the Amazon River to the sea.

Sunnier in the south

Quite the catch

Wake me up before you go go

Weenie or whale, I wonder?

I'm in the wrong part of town

Having a ball

Africa

Although Phoenician seafarers first sailed around Africa more than 2,600 years ago, the continent's interior was only fully explored in the 19th century. Explorers, including David Livingstone and Henry Morton Stanley, traced the course of the continent's great rivers, such as the Zambezi, the Congo, and the Nile.

Europe

The coasts of western Europe were explored in ancient times by Greek and Phoenician traders, who came to Britain to trade for tin. Later, from the 8th century CE, Vikings from Scandinavia set out across the North Sea and the Atlantic Ocean, discovering the Faroe Islands and Iceland.

Asia

The exploration of Asia was carried out by land, along the Silk Road. Created in about 100 BCE, this trade route linked China with the Middle East and the Mediterranean. The Silk Road was used by Chinese Buddhist pilgrims, who journeyed to India to study their religion, and also by medieval European travellers, such as Marco Polo.

Antarctica

The most southern continent, Antarctica is so far from inhabited lands that it was only discovered in the 1770s. The coastline was mapped in the 19th century. Between 1897 and 1917, there were 16 expeditions to Antarctica, sent by nine countries. The challenge to reach the South Pole was achieved in 1911 by Norwegian explorer Roald Amundsen.

Australasia

The first European explorers reached Australia in the 17th century. From the late 18th century onwards, the British settled on the southeast coasts, and went on to explore the interior.

Pacific Ocean

In the 16th century, European explorers first crossed the Pacific – the world's largest ocean. Later explorers discovered the ocean's scattered islands. They were astonished to find many inhabited by a single people, the Polynesians.

9

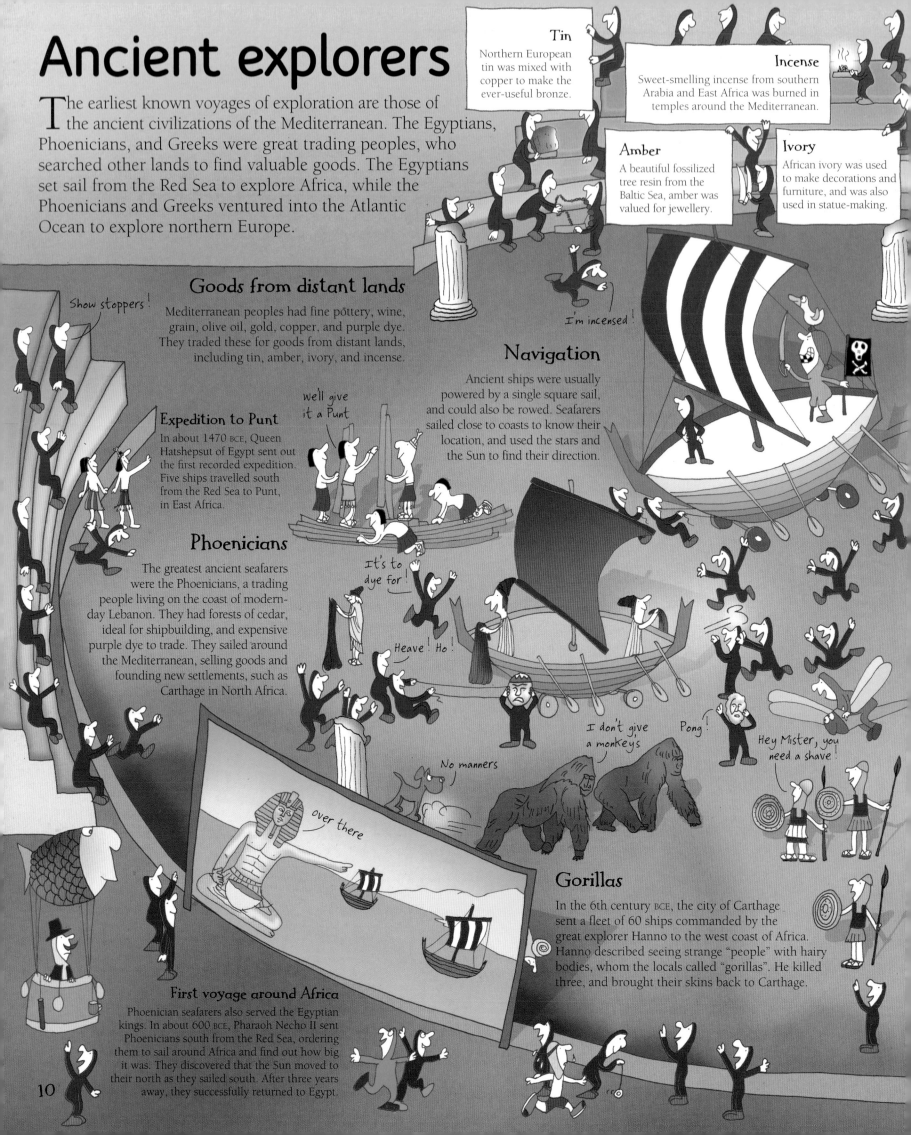

Ancient explorers

The earliest known voyages of exploration are those of the ancient civilizations of the Mediterranean. The Egyptians, Phoenicians, and Greeks were great trading peoples, who searched other lands to find valuable goods. The Egyptians set sail from the Red Sea to explore Africa, while the Phoenicians and Greeks ventured into the Atlantic Ocean to explore northern Europe.

Tin
Northern European tin was mixed with copper to make the ever-useful bronze.

Incense
Sweet-smelling incense from southern Arabia and East Africa was burned in temples around the Mediterranean.

Amber
A beautiful fossilized tree resin from the Baltic Sea, amber was valued for jewellery.

Ivory
African ivory was used to make decorations and furniture, and was also used in statue-making.

Goods from distant lands

Mediterranean peoples had fine pottery, wine, grain, olive oil, gold, copper, and purple dye. They traded these for goods from distant lands, including tin, amber, ivory, and incense.

Expedition to Punt

In about 1470 BCE, Queen Hatshepsut of Egypt sent out the first recorded expedition. Five ships travelled south from the Red Sea to Punt, in East Africa.

Phoenicians

The greatest ancient seafarers were the Phoenicians, a trading people living on the coast of modern-day Lebanon. They had forests of cedar, ideal for shipbuilding, and expensive purple dye to trade. They sailed around the Mediterranean, selling goods and founding new settlements, such as Carthage in North Africa.

Navigation

Ancient ships were usually powered by a single square sail, and could also be rowed. Seafarers sailed close to coasts to know their location, and used the stars and the Sun to find their direction.

First voyage around Africa

Phoenician seafarers also served the Egyptian kings. In about 600 BCE, Pharaoh Necho II sent Phoenicians south from the Red Sea, ordering them to sail around Africa and find out how big it was. They discovered that the Sun moved to their north as they sailed south. After three years away, they successfully returned to Egypt.

Gorillas

In the 6th century BCE, the city of Carthage sent a fleet of 60 ships commanded by the great explorer Hanno to the west coast of Africa. Hanno described seeing strange "people" with hairy bodies, whom the locals called "gorillas". He killed three, and brought their skins back to Carthage.

Alexander the Great

King Alexander the Great of Macedon was both a conqueror and an explorer. After conquering Persia, he led his army beyond the world known to the Greeks, invading India in 326 BCE.

Greek greats

Two Greek scientists contributed greatly to the ancient world's growing knowledge of Earth. Eratosthenes used mathematics to accurately calculate Earth's size, and the geographer Ptolemy made a hugely influential world map, which was the first to use lines of latitude and longitude to pinpoint locations.

Spinning sphere

As pioneers of science, the Greeks were the first to argue that the world is a sphere. Aristotle noticed that the stars seen in Egypt were different from those viewed further north. This showed that the surface of Earth must be curved.

Pytheas

The most famous Greek voyage of exploration was made in about 310 BCE, by Pytheas. He sailed north of Britain and reached a cold land he called Thule. This was probably Iceland or Norway.

Greek voyagers

The great seafaring rivals of the Phoenicians were the Ancient Greeks. From their homeland, the Greeks set out across the sea to found new cities, around the Mediterranean and Black Sea.

Sea monsters

In about 525 BCE, a Carthaginian called Himilco led an expedition beyond the Mediterranean, reaching the North Atlantic coasts of Europe. He reported seeing sea monsters, which were probably whales.

11

VIKING VOYAGES

The greatest seafarers of the early Middle Ages were the Vikings, the people of Scandinavia. From the late 8th century CE, they set off in all directions, to raid, trade, and settle new lands. They travelled east and south along the rivers of Russia to the Black Sea, as well as heading west into the North Sea and Atlantic Ocean. Here they found Iceland and Greenland, and became the first Europeans to reach North America.

Routes taken by Vikings c.790–1100 CE

Viking ships

Voyages were made in double-ended oak ships, with a single square sail. There were several types, but the best known was the longship, with a dragon figurehead. This slim, fast vessel was used in sea battles. For trading and exploring, people used a bigger bellied ship, called a "knarr".

Icelandic sagas

The stories of the Viking voyages of exploration were written down in Iceland, in books called sagas. These were composed for entertainment. On long, dark evenings, Icelanders loved to hear the stories of the voyages of their brave ancestors.

YOUR JOURNEY BEGINS THIS WAY

THE END

What a mystery

This is barking

It's been an ongoing saga

When will this story end?

Quite quackers

Who let you on board?

Where was Vinland?

Although Vinland must have been in North America, we do not know exactly where it was. The only Norse settlement that was discovered was in Newfoundland, but grapes do not grow there. Vinland may have been further south, where grapes could grow, or perhaps the Vikings mistook berries for grapes. They may have even made up the story to attract settlers.

Skraelings

In Vinland, the Viking settlers met native Americans, who they called "Skraelings". At first, these were friendly meetings, as the Vikings traded milk for animal skins. However, fighting later broke out. The Vikings had better weapons, but they were outnumbered, so they abandoned their settlement.

It's a long shot

Cripes!

Let's get outta here

Pick of the bunch

The green, green grass of home

Iceland

Floki Raven spent a cold winter in Iceland. He had failed to collect food for his livestock, so his animals starved to death. Disillusioned, he called the land "Iceland", which stuck. Despite the name, settlers were soon arriving.

Bird's-eye view

In the 860s, Iceland was reached by Floki Raven, who carried ravens on his ship to help with navigation. He would release each raven one by one. If a bird could not see land, it returned to the ship. Eventually one raven saw land and flew away, with Floki following.

Greenland

From Iceland, the Vikings sailed west, to another large, icy land. During the 980s, Erik the Red found an ice-free region on its west coast, and established a settlement there. To encourage settlers, Erik called this land "Greenland".

Helluland

Leif Erikson, the son of Erik the Red, sailed from Greenland in about 1000 CE. During this voyage of exploration, he reached a low land, which resembled a single slab of rock. Leif named it Helluland (meaning "Slab land"). Sailing south, he came to a forested region he called Markland (meaning "Wood land").

Vinland

After two days further sailing, Leif reached a land with fine grazing and plenty of salmon. His men built houses and spent the winter there. They were delighted with the mild climate. They also found wild grapes, so Leif named it Vinland (meaning "Wine land"). Leif and his men had become the first Europeans to visit North America.

13

Travellers' tales

In the Middle Ages, long-distance travel was difficult and dangerous for Europeans trying to reach Asia or Africa. With only vague ideas of these distant lands, people loved hearing stories about the strange customs of foreigners. Some tales were written by genuine travellers, such as Friar John of Piano Carpini, the first European to reach Mongolia. Others, including stories of dog-headed men and gold-mining ants, were wild inventions of the imagination.

John of Piano Carpini

The Pope's ambassador was Friar John of Piano Carpini. He was about 65 years old and so overweight that he had trouble walking. Thanks to a number of horses supplied by the Mongols, he managed to travel 4,800 km (3,000 miles) in 106 days, arriving at the court of their new ruler Guyuk Khan.

Mongol Empire

By the 1240s, the Mongols had conquered a huge empire stretching from China to southern Russia. In 1241, their armies briefly invaded central Europe. Pope Innocent IV wanted to learn as much as possible about the Mongol threat. In 1245, he sent a mission to their court.

Genghis Khan

During the 1220s, Christians in Europe learned that their Muslim enemies in Asia were under attack from a powerful eastern king. People wondered if this was Prester John. In fact, it was Genghis Khan, ruler of the warlike Mongols from East Asia.

Prester John

One story told of a powerful Christian ruler called Prester John who lived somewhere in Asia or Africa. He was said to be so rich that his servants were kings in their own right. Europeans dreamed of finding him, and winning his help in their wars.

Giddy up!

Give over!

Roll up, roll up

Oh no, I've got vertigo!

Ready for the curtain call?

No photography, thank you

You don't scare me

Smile nicely, Mongols

Less pies for you, John

Armed and dangerous

King Khan

Khan I join you?

He rules

Hello, your highness

ENTRANCE

Welcome to my circus

Yippee

Haven't seen you two in a while

TRAVELLING CIRCUS

oh, what a circus

Here's the slippery slope

Friar John's journey

The Mongols seemed savage and terrifying to Friar John. On his journey, he saw many signs of recent Mongol destruction, such as heaps of human bones, deserted towns, and ruined castles. Guyuk Khan told him it was the Mongols' mission to rule the world.

William of Rubruck

In 1253, King Louis IX of France sent another friar, William of Rubruck, to see if the Mongols could be converted to the Christian religion. Although William failed to convert them, he wrote a wonderful book describing Mongol customs, including their clothing, diet, and religious beliefs.

A guaranteed bestseller

Just a flying visit?

Dem bones, dem bones

There are no funny bones

What a load of baloney

Stop interrupting

Smelly foot

Put your best foot forward

It's bigfoot

Sir John Mandeville

The most popular medieval travel book was *The Travels of Sir John Mandeville*, written in the 1350s. Its author claimed to be an English knight who had travelled across Asia. In reality, the stories were mostly made up, or copied from earlier books.

Giant foot folk

Inside Sir John Mandeville's book were descriptions of an island where the inhabitants each had one enormous foot. During the hottest part of the day, they would lie on their backs, using their giant feet as sunshades!

You look ruff

He's a bit mouthy

Tall story

Gold-mining ants

According to Sir John Mandeville, Ceylon (Sri Lanka) was inhabited by ants as big as dogs. The ants spent their days mining for gold, which was found there in vast quantities. This was a very old story, first told in the 5th century BCE by the Ancient Greek writer Herodotus.

Enough of your antics

Island monsters

Sir John Mandeville wrote of islands off Asia that were home to dog-headed men, and people without heads, who had eyes in each shoulder and mouths in the middle of their chests!

It's a minefield that way

Polo's passport

The Khan grew fond of Polo, who learned the Mongol language and told entertaining stories. As a reward, he gave Polo a gold passport, so he could travel freely within his empire.

Better check your passport's valid

He looks a fiery fellow

Khan's Palace

After three years, the Polos reached Kublai Khan's Palace, in Khanbalik (modern-day Beijing). The walls were covered with gold and silver, and decorated with pictures of dragons.

Do you hear something?

only the camel's tummy rumbling

Gobi Desert

The Polos then crossed the vast Gobi Desert, a difficult journey which took them 30 days. The desert was said to be haunted and, at night, strange voices could be heard.

Brrr ....

Pamir Mountains

In central Asia, the Polos crossed the snow-capped Pamir Mountains, which stretch between Afghanistan and China. These are so high that they are nicknamed the "roof of the world".

START

A slow start

This is just the beginning

Silk Road start

In 1271, the 17-year-old Marco Polo set off with his father and uncle, both merchants who had visited China. They travelled on the Silk Road, the trade route between China and the West.

Paper money

Polo was amazed to find that the Chinese used paper money, made from the bark of the mulberry tree. Paper was a Chinese invention. At the time, Europeans used metal coins.

A Polo mint

Can't buy me love

Dangerous animals

In addition to China, Polo visited Burma, Malaya, and India. He was surprised by the quantities of spices, such as pepper and ginger, grown here. He also saw dangerous animals, such as lions, tigers, and bears.

I can't bear having visitors

Asbestos and coal

In China, Polo saw a fire-resistant material, which he called "salamander" (asbestos). This was mined from mountains and spun into cloth. He also saw coal, which was not yet used as a fuel in Europe.

It's all mine!

Fab fuel

MARCO POLO

The most famous medieval European traveller was Italian Marco Polo. After travelling east along the Silk Road, he reached the court of Kublai Khan, the Mongol ruler of China. Polo spent 17 years travelling around China and other parts of Asia. He returned to Europe after 24 years away, and described the wonders he had seen in a book. His reports of wealth in Asia inspired other explorers, such as Christopher Columbus, to find a way there.

AFRICA

EUROPE

Venice

INDIAN OCEAN

ASIA

INDIA

MALAYA

BURMA

CHINA

Pamir Mountains

Gobi Desert

Beijing

— Marco Polo's route (1271–95)

Imperial Post

Polo was impressed by the efficiency of the Chinese Imperial Post. Along the roads of the Khan's empire were 10,000 posting stations, with 200,000 horses, so messengers could carry letters.

Express delivery of cooourse

Really, Marco?

Taken prisoner

Back home in the Italian city of Venice, Polo joined a Venetian fleet fighting the Genoese in 1298. He was captured and imprisoned with a writer, Rustichello of Pisa, who recorded Polo's stories.

I get bored of listening

Supreme storyteller

Thinking Polo's stories were exaggerated, people asked him, on his deathbed, to admit that he was making things up. Polo replied that he hadn't told half of all he'd seen!

Night, fellas

Tell us some more

END

IBN BATTUTA

The greatest traveller of the Middle Ages was Ibn Battuta, a Moroccan Muslim. It was the goal of every Muslim to visit the holy cities of Mecca and Medina, in Arabia. After setting off on his pilgrimage, Battuta found that he loved travelling to new lands. For almost 30 years, he journeyed through Asia and Africa. He covered at least 120,000 km (75,000 miles), making an effort never to use the same road twice.

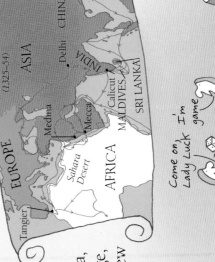

Strong start

In 1325, Ibn Battuta set off for Mecca and Medina. He travelled alone, riding on a donkey. For safety, he joined a caravan of fellow pilgrims. By the time it reached Egypt, his caravan was several thousand strong.

Hyena heist

Crossing the Egyptian desert, Battuta's caravan encountered hyenas. Battuta stayed awake all night to drive them away. One hyena took a bag of dates from his bag, and ran off with it!

Holy cities

When Battuta reached Mecca and Medina, he met Muslims from many lands. He heard there were opportunities for Muslim scholars in India, and after a few years of travel, he decided to go.

Home at last

Battuta had many more adventures, including trips to China, Spain, and East and West Africa. In 1354, he returned home to Morocco, where he told his amazing travel stories to a scribe.

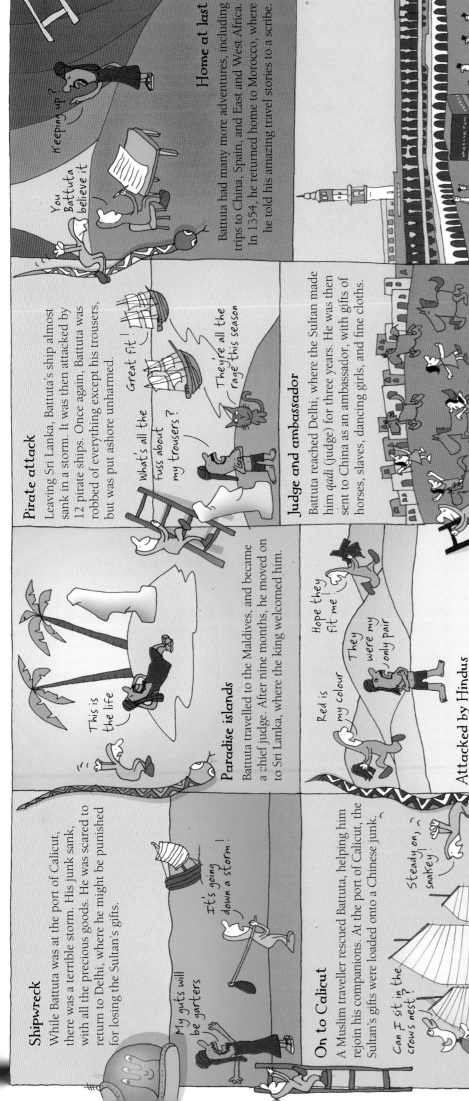

Pirate attack

Leaving Sri Lanka, Battuta's ship almost sank in a storm. It was then attacked by 12 pirate ships. Once again, Battuta was robbed of everything except his trousers, but was put ashore unharmed.

Paradise islands

Battuta travelled to the Maldives, and became a chief judge. After nine months, he moved on to Sri Lanka, where the king welcomed him.

Judge and ambassador

Battuta reached Delhi, where the Sultan made him *qadi* (judge) for three years. He was then sent to China as an ambassador, with gifts of horses, slaves, dancing girls, and fine cloths.

Shipwreck

While Battuta was at the port of Calicut, there was a terrible storm. His junk sank, with all the precious goods. He was scared to return to Delhi, where he might be punished for losing the Sultan's gifts.

On to Calicut

A Muslim traveller rescued Battuta, helping him rejoin his companions. At the port of Calicut, the Sultan's gifts were loaded onto a Chinese junk.

Attacked by Hindus

Battuta set off with the gifts from the Sultan for the Chinese Emperor. Soon after, Battuta became separated from his party. He was captured by 40 Hindus, who robbed him of all his personal belongings except his trousers.

Chinese explorers

At various points in history, the Chinese set off on journeys of exploration – travelling overland to the West and by sea as far as East Africa. These journeys were exceptional events. The Chinese saw their homeland, called the "Middle Kingdom", as the centre of the world, and they looked down on foreigners as savages. As a result, they usually had little interest in exploring other lands.

Zhang Qian

The earliest known Chinese explorer was Zhang Qian, who was sent by Emperor Wu to the rulers of Central Asia in 138 BCE. After 13 years away, Qian returned home with stories of the amazing lands he had visited.

The Silk Road

Zhang Qian's journey led to new trade links between China and the West, using a route called the "Silk Road". From China, merchants travelled west, carrying Chinese silks, which they traded for western products, such as grapes, walnuts, and flax.

Buddhist pilgrims

Following contact with the West, many Chinese people adopted a new religion called Buddhism. From the 4th century CE, Chinese Buddhist monks travelled to India to study their religion in its homeland. The earliest known Buddhist pilgrim was Fa Xian, who set off along the Silk Road in 399 CE.

Mighty Ming

Chinese power was at its height under Emperor Yongle of the Ming dynasty, who ruled between 1402–24. To increase Chinese influence, he sent out six huge naval expeditions to the western ocean, commanded by his admiral, Zheng He.

Chinese fleet

On his first voyage in 1405, Zheng He led a fleet of more than 200 ships, carrying about 27,000 men. The fleet included 62 great "treasure ships". The largest of these were approximately 120 m (400 ft) long and 50 m (160 ft) wide.

18

Spectacular seas

Back in China, Zheng He set up a tablet on which he wrote, "We have crossed immense water spaces and have seen in the ocean huge waves like mountains rising in the sky".

ASIA

ARABIA

INDIA

THAILAND

AFRICA

INDIAN OCEAN

INDONESIA

Voyages of Zheng He

Shipshape messages

The crew members of Zheng He's ships passed messages to each other using flags, lanterns, bells, carrier pigeons, gongs, and banners. As the ships arrived in distant lands, they must have presented a spectacular sight.

That's the way

Just getting into the swing of things

Compass

Zheng He used the compass – a Chinese invention – to find his way. This was a spoon made of a magnetic mineral, balanced on a plate. The spoon's changing position showed the direction the ship was going.

Spoon

Plate

Two birds in the hand

What a cat-astrophe!

Great gifts

Zheng He's fleet visited Thailand, Indonesia, India, Arabia, and East Africa. He gave presents to local rulers, such as Ming vases, gold, silver, porcelain, and silk. In exchange, the rulers presented him with ivory, pearls, spices, and unusual animals and birds, including ostriches, lions, and zebras.

It's the golden age

So much junk

Miaow for now

It's a motley crew

Giraffe

The strangest animal Zheng He brought back was an East African giraffe, a gift for the emperor's private zoo.

Not my usual neck of the woods

Junk sails

Chinese ships, called junks, had large sails stiffened with strips of bamboo. Unlike the square sails of European ships, these could be placed at different angles, allowing a junk to sail into the wind.

We're sailing close to the wind

Blowin' in the wind

I love junk food

Wish this was a speedboat

Should I be looking more stern?

Don't chew with your mouth open

19

Henry the Navigator

The great European Age of Exploration was started in the 15th century by Prince Henry of Portugal, nicknamed "the Navigator". He was made governor of the southernmost part of Portugal in 1419, and sent out ships commanded by his household nobles to explore the Atlantic Ocean and the African coast. His court resembled a school for explorers, where new maps were made, and scientists and sea captains exchanged ideas about navigation.

It's plain sailing from now on

SAILING SCHOOL

Shiver his timbers

I wish he wood go away

Caravel

The Portuguese developed a new kind of ship, called a caravel. It had lateen (triangular) sails instead of square ones. This made it better at sailing into the wind, by "tacking" (sailing in a zigzag line).

Winds

The prevailing wind off the coast of Portugal blows southwest, perfect for taking ships down the coast of Africa. Portuguese caravels could sail by the west African coast with the wind behind them, and then return home by tacking against it.

North Atlantic wind blows in a clockwise circle

PORTUGAL · EUROPE

Well, blow me over

AFRICA

Anticlockwise current

On the cape

At first, Henry's sailors were scared of the unknown. Until 1434, they refused to pass a point called Cape Bojador, afraid that they would be unable to get home again.

Sew what?

Ripping yarn

Currents

As they sailed south, the Portuguese explorers learned about the Atlantic Ocean's water currents, as well as its winds. In the South Atlantic, the current flows in a great anticlockwise circle, up the coast of Africa, and then out to the west.

Scaredy cats

ENTRANCE

I'm not too cool for school

Cape Bojador

AFRICA

Here's where we fear to thread

It's a current affair

Hi, Henry

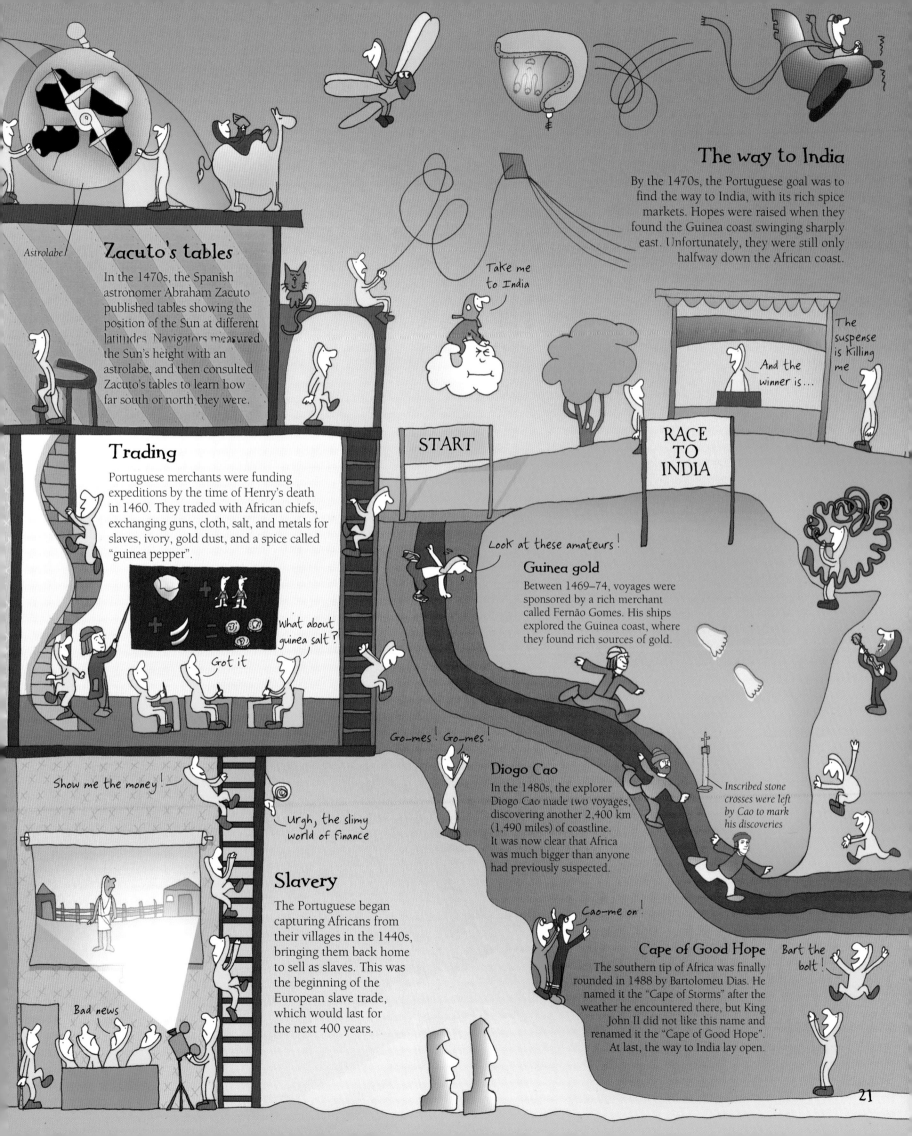

Zacuto's tables

Astrolabe

In the 1470s, the Spanish astronomer Abraham Zacuto published tables showing the position of the Sun at different latitudes. Navigators measured the Sun's height with an astrolabe, and then consulted Zacuto's tables to learn how far south or north they were.

Trading

Portuguese merchants were funding expeditions by the time of Henry's death in 1460. They traded with African chiefs, exchanging guns, cloth, salt, and metals for slaves, ivory, gold dust, and a spice called "guinea pepper".

Got it

What about guinea salt?

Slavery

The Portuguese began capturing Africans from their villages in the 1440s, bringing them back home to sell as slaves. This was the beginning of the European slave trade, which would last for the next 400 years.

Show me the money!

Urgh, the slimy world of finance

Bad news

The way to India

By the 1470s, the Portuguese goal was to find the way to India, with its rich spice markets. Hopes were raised when they found the Guinea coast swinging sharply east. Unfortunately, they were still only halfway down the African coast.

Take me to India

And the winner is...

The suspense is killing me

START

RACE TO INDIA

Look at these amateurs!

Guinea gold

Between 1469–74, voyages were sponsored by a rich merchant called Fernão Gomes. His ships explored the Guinea coast, where they found rich sources of gold.

Go-mes! Go-mes!

Diogo Cao

In the 1480s, the explorer Diogo Cao made two voyages, discovering another 2,400 km (1,490 miles) of coastline. It was now clear that Africa was much bigger than anyone had previously suspected.

Inscribed stone crosses were left by Cao to mark his discoveries

Cao-me on!

Cape of Good Hope

The southern tip of Africa was finally rounded in 1488 by Bartolomeu Dias. He named it the "Cape of Storms" after the weather he encountered there, but King John II did not like this name and renamed it the "Cape of Good Hope". At last, the way to India lay open.

Bart the bolt!

On to India

Following Bartolomeu Dias's rounding of South Africa, the route to India lay open. In 1497, King Manuel I of Portugal decided to send an expedition there, led by a young nobleman, called Vasco da Gama. King Manuel hoped that da Gama would return with valuable spices, and also with news of Christian rulers said to be living in India. On 8 July that year, da Gama set off on his great voyage, with four ships and 170 men.

Sturdy ships

Two of da Gama's ships were specially built for the voyage. These were not caravels but larger ships, called carracks. Unlike caravals, they had square sails, which would prove easier to handle in the rough weather of the South Atlantic.

FILM STUDIO ENTRANCE

Weighty goods

The ships were loaded with enough supplies for a three-year voyage. There were casks of wine, salted beef and pork, and weapons and ammunition. Trade goods, to exchange for Indian spices, included jars of honey, woollen hats, and coral beads.

Into the Atlantic

Instead of following the coast of Africa, like previous explorers, the ships sailed southwest, out into the ocean. Da Gama was using the wind system of the South Atlantic, which blows in an anti-clockwise circle. He would have the wind blowing behind him during his journey.

Land at last!

Da Gama's ships spent a worrying 13 weeks out of sight of land. When the explorers finally saw the coast of Africa, in November 1497, they celebrated by decorating their ships with flags, firing guns, and putting on their best clothes.

SILENCE ON SET: FILMING IN PROGRESS

PORTUGAL
ASIA
AFRICA
INDIA
Goa
Calicut
Malindi
Mombasa
INDIAN
OCEAN
Mozambique
BRAZIL
AUSTRALIA

—— Da Gama (1487–88)
—— Cabral (1500)

Accidental find

Da Gama's voyage was followed up quickly. In 1500, fellow Portugese navigator Pedro Cabral sailed to India with a fleet of 13 well-armed ships. On the way, he accidentally discovered Brazil, and claimed it for Portugal. Cabral returned with ships loaded with spices and rubies.

No

Will they invite me to the premiere?

Pedro leads the life!

A box office smash

Return journey

On his return journey, da Gama made the mistake of sailing against the monsoon wind. Crossing the Indian Ocean took four months, and almost half his men died of scurvy, caused by lack of fresh food. In September 1499, he returned to Portugal, his ships loaded with spices.

Wait up!

Saint Shiva

The Portuguese had never seen Hindus before. They were amazed by their colourful temples, with statues of strange-looking gods, such as Shiva. Da Gama knew that Muslims and Jews did not worship statues. He mistakenly thought the Indian people were Christians, and that Shiva was a saint.

Trade port

On 20 May 1498, the fleet reached Calicut, a busy port on the Indian coast. The wealthy ruler, the Samorin, was not impressed by the Portuguese, who had brought no expensive gifts for him. Despite this, he allowed them to trade.

Slow down

Less haste, more speed

What goodies do you have for me?

What a terrible noise

Take 267

This is your pilot speaking

Action!

New navigator

In Malindi, da Gama was lucky to hire an Arab pilot, who offered to show him the way to India. This meant sailing with the seasonal monsoon wind, which blows to the northeast in summer and switches direction in winter.

Unwelcome visitor

Da Gama sailed on into the Indian Ocean, where no European ships had gone before. In East Africa, he visited three Muslim ports – Mozambique, Mombasa, and Malindi. Local rulers did not welcome Christians, nor their trade goods.

23

Sailing west

Christopher Columbus was an Italian seafarer, who read about the wealth of Asia from Marco Polo's book. It struck him that the quickest sea route was not south around Africa, but west across the Atlantic Ocean, believing Asia to be on the other side. He was wrong, but his voyages led to the discovery of a great continent between Europe and Asia, later called America.

Searching for a sponsor

After being turned down by the Portuguese king in 1484, Columbus moved to Spain. He promised King Ferdinand and Queen Isabella that his voyage would make them rich, and spread the Christian faith to Asia. In 1492, they agreed to sponsor his plans, and Columbus started his preparations.

Setting sail

On 3 August 1492, Columbus set sail with 90 men on board three ships – *Santa Maria*, *Pinta*, and *Niña*. They sailed southwest to the Canary Islands, as Columbus believed that Japan lay west of this point. He knew that the winds there usually blew to the west, and would therefore help him across.

You need to cool off

All aboard the Colum-bus!

Water way to paint!

Dead reckoning

Columbus navigated by "dead reckoning" – keeping track of his ship's direction and the distance it travelled. To calculate the distance, Columbus had to keep a record of the speed of his ship over a set period of time.

Sargasso Sea

On 16 September, the ships found themselves sailing through a mass of bright green seaweed, covered with crabs. The sailors were excited by this, thinking land was near. In fact, they had discovered the Sargasso Sea, a vast area of floating weed in the middle of the Atlantic.

He's making a show of us!

Don't go!

Near mutiny

As they sailed further away from land, the men grew increasingly worried. On 10 October, the crew of *Santa Maria* demanded that Columbus give up his foolish plan and take them home, but he refused to give in to their demands.

All I sea are weeds!

Boo hiss!

Magnetic compass points to north

Right direction
To find his direction, Columbus used a magnetic compass.

Sandglass
He measured time using a sandglass, which he turned over after every half hour.

Speed
To estimate speed, he threw chips of wood over the side, seeing how fast the ship passed them.

Chart
At regular intervals, Columbus marked the course he had travelled on a chart.

Don't be so crabby

They're staging a protest!

Land ahoy!

At last, land was sighted on 12 October. Columbus had reached the Bahamas. Going ashore, he was welcomed by astonished but friendly people. Thinking that he had reached the Indies (Asia), Columbus mistakenly called them "Indians". As a result of this error, native Americans are still called Indians today.

Homecoming

Columbus returned to Spain in March 1493, bringing captured natives, colourful parrots, and strange foods, including maize and pineapples. The delighted monarchs rewarded him with the title "Admiral of the Ocean Sea". They asked him to lead a new expedition, to found a Spanish colony in Hispaniola.

Islands explored

Columbus sailed on, exploring the coasts of Cuba and Haiti, which he called "Hispaniola" (the Spanish island). He thought that Hispaniola would be a perfect place for a Spanish settlement. Nothing Columbus saw matched Marco Polo's descriptions of Asia, but he was still sure that Japan was nearby.

Voyaging on

Columbus made three more voyages, exploring the coasts of the South and Central American mainland. He decided that he must have reached the "Earthly paradise", described in the Bible.

The voyages of Christopher Columbus
- 1st voyage (1492–93)
- 2nd voyage (1493–96)
- 3rd voyage (1498–1500)
- 4th voyage (1502–04)

NORTH AMERICA
ATLANTIC OCEAN
NEWFOUNDLAND
BAHAMAS
CUBA
HISPANIOLA
SOUTH AMERICA
EUROPE
AFRICA

John Cabot

Soon other explorers were crossing the Atlantic. In 1497, John Cabot, an Italian sailor living in England, made a northern crossing and reached Newfoundland. Like Columbus, he believed he was in Asia.

A new world

An Italian named Amerigo Vespucci explored the mainland in 1499 and 1501. He argued that it was not part of Asia, but a "new world". The mapmaker Martin Waldseemuller suggested naming it "America" in his honour, and it has stuck to this day.

AROUND THE WORLD

Like Christopher Columbus before him, Portuguese nobleman Ferdinand Magellan believed that a western route to Asia would be quicker than the eastern one used by the Portuguese. He needed to find a passage of water through America, but mistakenly assumed that Asia must be only a short distance further. Although Magellan did not complete his journey, the expedition he commanded resulted in the very first voyage around the world.

START

THIS WAY

Elcano

Magellan

Spooky!

Rebel rebel

Help!

Man overboard!

Do you smell cheese?

We're shipping off

Storms ahead!

Let's seal it with a kiss

Tight squeeze

Keep on the strait and narrow

AROUND THE WORLD RIDE

Setting off

Magellan's first voyages were to Asia and for the king of Portugal. When Magellan moved to Spain, he won backing for his western-route plan from King Charles I. On 20 September 1519, he set off with a fleet of five ships, carrying about 265 men, including Spaniard Juan Sebastián Elcano.

In South America

After sailing down the side of South America, Magellan spent the winter on the coast. His Spanish captains disliked taking orders from a foreigner, so they mutinied (rebelled). Magellan had one captain executed and two others marooned (left behind).

Big Foot Land

Magellan named the southernmost part of South America *Patagonia* ("Big Foot land"), after the tall native Americans he saw living there. One of his ships was wrecked in Patagonia, though its crew was rescued.

Sailing through the strait

In October 1520, Magellan finally found a strait (passage of water) through South America. One ship deserted the expedition and sailed back to Spain, leaving Magellan with just three. It took them a difficult 38 days to sail through the strait, which was later named after him.

World's first

On reaching Spain, on 6 September 1522, after his three-year voyage, Elcano had completed the first journey around the world. King Charles V awarded him a coat of arms. It was a globe with the motto, "You went around me first".

Returning home

On the homeward journey, *Trinidad* was left behind due to damage caused during the voyage. Only *Victoria* returned to Spain, with just 18 survivors, all sick with scurvy. Yet the ship's cargo of cloves meant that the expedition had still made an excellent profit.

The Spice Islands

With too few men to crew their three ships, one was abandoned. Under a new commander, Juan Sebastián Elcano, the two ships, called *Trinidad* and *Victoria*, sailed on to the Moluccas (Spice Islands). Here they loaded up with cloves and other spices.

Fatal Philippines

In March 1521, Magellan finally reached the Philippines, where he and his men were involved in a local war. During a battle on Mactan Island, the locals attacked them with swords and bamboo spears. Magellan and several of his men were killed.

Pacific crossing

Magellan's ships spent four months in the open sea. Food supplies ran low, and the men fell ill with scurvy, due to a lack of vitamin C. They were so hungry that they ate leather and sawdust, and rats were sold for gold coins.

Peaceful Ocean

The expedition then sailed into an ocean. Impressed by the sea's calmness, Magellan named it the *Mar Pacifico* (Peaceful Ocean). He expected to reach the Indies in a short time. In fact, he had entered the world's largest ocean, which covers a third of the planet's surface.

27

SPANISH CONQUISTADORES

In the early 16th century, Spanish explorers learned that the American mainland was home to wealthy civilizations, rich in gold and silver. The two great empires were the Aztecs in Mexico and the Incas in Peru. The Spaniards set out to conquer these peoples, with the advantage of guns, horses, steel swords, and armour. Though there were greater numbers of Aztecs and Incas, they had only stone-bladed weapons.

Moctezuma

The Aztec ruler, Moctezuma, heard that strange metal-wearing beings had arrived on the coast. He did not know if they were gods or men. Too scared to attack the Spaniards, Moctezuma sent presents to Cortés.

In Tenochtitlan

Cortés marched to Tenochtitlan, forging alliances with Mexican peoples who hated their Aztec rulers. Although Moctezuma welcomed Cortés, the Spaniards then took the emperor prisoner, using him to give their orders to the Aztecs.

Final conquest

In May 1520, the Aztecs rose up against the Spanish, and drove them out of Tenochtitlan. However, Cortés gathered a new army from Cuba and, helped by his Mexican allies, came back to conquer the city three months later.

Sacrifice

The Aztecs would occasionally use a prisoner as a ritual sacrifice to their gods. In battle, they did not try to kill enemies, but to capture them alive. This would be a disadvantage when fighting the Spanish.

Ready to conquer

In 1519, Hernán Cortés, a Spanish settler in Cuba, led an expedition of 11 ships with about 500 men to the coast of Mexico. He realized that he had discovered a wealthy empire, and resolved to conquer it.

The Aztecs

The empire of this warlike people stretched all the way from the Pacific Ocean to the Gulf of Mexico. Their capital, Tenochtitlan, was dominated by tall pyramid temples, where prisoners were offered as sacrifices to Aztec gods.

Map labels: NORTH AMERICA, GULF OF MEXICO, CUBA, CARIBBEAN SEA, Tenochtitlan

■ Aztec Empire
— Hernán Cortés's route to Tenochtitlan (1519)

Speech/sign labels: It's all downhill from here • DOWN • FURTHER DOWN • I'm feeling down • Are metallics in this season? • Fetching feathers! • Try a pedicure • Scaredy cat • Didn't you like the gifts? • Seize him! • UP A BIT! • on the up • Is this my best side? • The camera never lies • This is the ultimate sacrifice • It's a rich man's world • Hang in there • You're being a bit defensive • Who hired the singer? • Give peace a chance • UPWARDS

28

Sapa Inca

The Inca Empire was a well-organized state, ruled by the Sapa Inca (sole lord), who was seen as a child of the Sun, and worshipped as a living god. When Pizarro arrived in Peru, the empire was ruled by Atahualpa.

Following fortune

In 1519, a tough former soldier called Francisco Pizarro was living in Panama. When he heard of a wealthy civilization in South America, he prepared an expedition. In 1531, he set sail for Peru with three ships, 185 men, and 27 horses.

The Incas

From their homeland high in the Andes Mountains, the Incas conquered a vast empire, that was home to more than 12 million people. Expert builders, the Incas constructed a network of roads and stone-lined terraces for farming.

PACIFIC OCEAN

SOUTH AMERICA

Andes Mountains

Panama

■ Inca Empire
— Francisco Pizarro's route (1531–33)

Atahualpa

Pizarro led his men inland to see Atahualpa, who was stationed with his army. The Inca leader agreed to meet Pizarro. He did not think the Spaniards were gods, and he did not fear them, as their numbers were so few.

Seizing the ruler

At their meeting, on 16 November 1532, Pizarro's men made a surprise attack on Atahualpa's army. They fired a cannon and charged at his guards with their steel swords. Within minutes, the shocked Inca leader was the prisoner of the Spaniards.

Broken promise

Pizarro promised to free the Inca leader if he filled a large room with gold and silver. Atahualpa sent out orders and the room was filled up. Instead of keeping his word, Pizarro had Atahualpa strangled. The Spaniards took over his empire, though the Incas were not conquered completely until the 1570s.

OLD AND NEW WORLDS

Before 1492, there had been virtually no contact between "the Old World" (Eurasia and Africa) and "the New World" (the Americas). Each had its own distinctive animals, ideas, and technologies. Following Christopher Columbus's voyage across the Atlantic Ocean in 1492, the two worlds were brought together. This "Columbian Exchange" involved people, animals, ideas, and diseases crossing between the two in both directions, and it changed the lives of everyone.

OLD WORLD MARKET

NEW WORLD MARKET

Diseases

European settlers brought many new diseases to the Americas, including smallpox, influenza, measles, chickenpox, and typhus. Native Americans, who had no resistance to these diseases, died in vast numbers. As the diseases spread, about 80 per cent of the native population was wiped out.

African slaves

So many native Americans died from new diseases that the European conquerors did not have enough people to work on their lands. From the 16th to the 19th centuries, about ten million African slaves were shipped over to the Americas.

Foods

Across the world, people benefited from new food plants. The New World received wheat, oats, barley, coffee, tea, sugar, rice, and onions. Meanwhile, the Old World gained maize, potatoes, tomatoes, chilli peppers, pineapples, peanuts, and chocolate.

Pesky Pests

Carried in the holds of ships, pests passed in both directions between the Old and New Worlds. Brown rats and cockroaches, which spread many diseases, moved from Europe to the Americas. The North American Colorado Beetle can wipe out potato crops, and in the 19th century it spread across much of Europe and Asia.

Manioc

One of the most useful discoveries was the food plant manioc, also known as cassava, found by Christopher Columbus in South America. Manioc resists drought and pests, and grows well even in poor soil. It is now eaten in tropical regions, from Africa to Southeast Asia.

Old World animals

The Old World had many more domesticated animals than the New World. The most important were horses, sheep, pigs, and chickens, which were all introduced to the Americas. The Plains Indians of North America became expert horse riders, using their new animals to hunt buffalo.

New World animals

When New World animals came to Europe, they were often given incorrect names, because people got confused about where they really came from. The Turkey bird actually came from Mexico, the Guinea pig from Peru, and the Muscovy (Moscow) duck from Central and South America.

Metal technology

Before 1492, native Americans only used softer metals (gold, silver, and copper), which were suitable for ornaments. The Europeans introduced harder metals (iron, steel, and bronze) to the Americas. These were ideal for tools, such as ploughs, and weapons, including steel swords and guns.

Wheeled transport

Europeans introduced wheeled transport, pulled by horses and oxen, to the Americas. Native people had never invented carts, perhaps because they had no animals strong enough to pull them. Although they knew about the wheel, they only used it to make pull-along toys.

Languages and religion

Many native American languages died out, as people learned to speak English, French, Spanish, and Portuguese – the languages of their conquerors. The Europeans also brought Christianity, which became the main religion across the Americas. Worship of the old Inca and Aztec gods was banned.

31

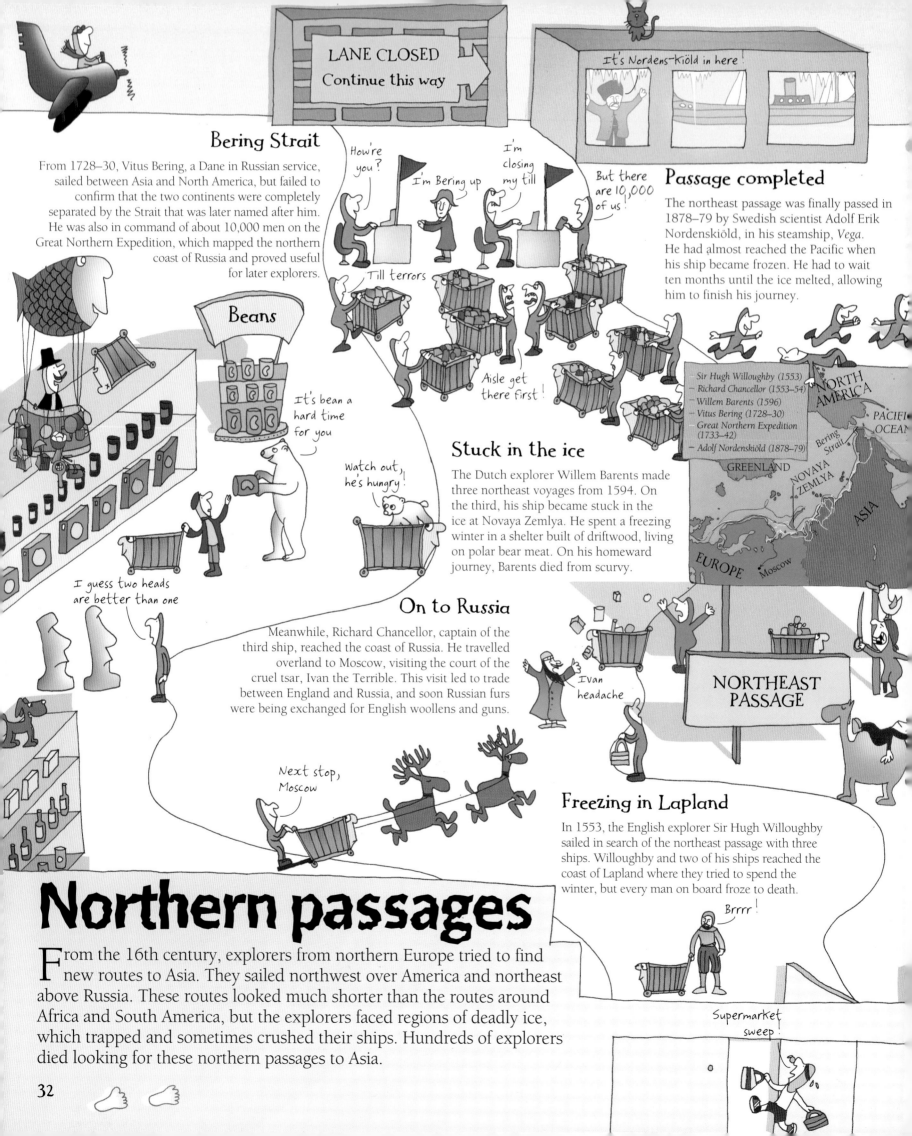

Bering Strait

From 1728–30, Vitus Bering, a Dane in Russian service, sailed between Asia and North America, but failed to confirm that the two continents were completely separated by the Strait that was later named after him. He was also in command of about 10,000 men on the Great Northern Expedition, which mapped the northern coast of Russia and proved useful for later explorers.

Passage completed

The northeast passage was finally passed in 1878–79 by Swedish scientist Adolf Erik Nordenskiöld, in his steamship, *Vega*. He had almost reached the Pacific when his ship became frozen. He had to wait ten months until the ice melted, allowing him to finish his journey.

Stuck in the ice

The Dutch explorer Willem Barents made three northeast voyages from 1594. On the third, his ship became stuck in the ice at Novaya Zemlya. He spent a freezing winter in a shelter built of driftwood, living on polar bear meat. On his homeward journey, Barents died from scurvy.

On to Russia

Meanwhile, Richard Chancellor, captain of the third ship, reached the coast of Russia. He travelled overland to Moscow, visiting the court of the cruel tsar, Ivan the Terrible. This visit led to trade between England and Russia, and soon Russian furs were being exchanged for English woollens and guns.

Freezing in Lapland

In 1553, the English explorer Sir Hugh Willoughby sailed in search of the northeast passage with three ships. Willoughby and two of his ships reached the coast of Lapland where they tried to spend the winter, but every man on board froze to death.

- Sir Hugh Willoughby (1553)
- Richard Chancellor (1553–54)
- Willem Barents (1596)
- Vitus Bering (1728–30)
- Great Northern Expedition (1733–42)
- Adolf Nordenskiöld (1878–79)

Northern passages

From the 16th century, explorers from northern Europe tried to find new routes to Asia. They sailed northwest over America and northeast above Russia. These routes looked much shorter than the routes around Africa and South America, but the explorers faced regions of deadly ice, which trapped and sometimes crushed their ships. Hundreds of explorers died looking for these northern passages to Asia.

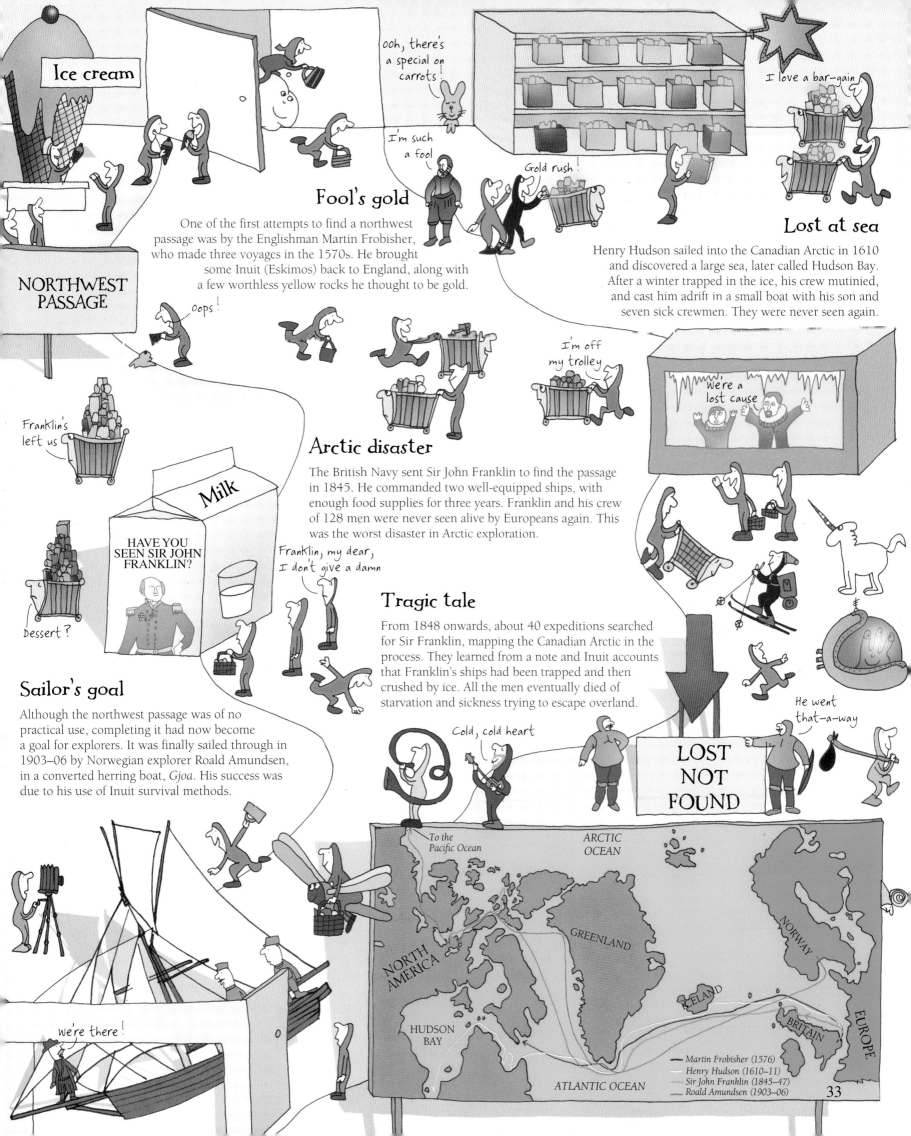

Ice cream

ooh, there's a special on carrots!

I love a bar-gain

I'm such a fool

Gold rush!

Fool's gold

One of the first attempts to find a northwest passage was by the Englishman Martin Frobisher, who made three voyages in the 1570s. He brought some Inuit (Eskimos) back to England, along with a few worthless yellow rocks he thought to be gold.

Lost at sea

Henry Hudson sailed into the Canadian Arctic in 1610 and discovered a large sea, later called Hudson Bay. After a winter trapped in the ice, his crew mutinied, and cast him adrift in a small boat with his son and seven sick crewmen. They were never seen again.

NORTHWEST PASSAGE

oops!

Franklin's left us

I'm off my trolley

we're a lost cause

Arctic disaster

The British Navy sent Sir John Franklin to find the passage in 1845. He commanded two well-equipped ships, with enough food supplies for three years. Franklin and his crew of 128 men were never seen alive by Europeans again. This was the worst disaster in Arctic exploration.

Milk

HAVE YOU SEEN SIR JOHN FRANKLIN?

Franklin, my dear, I don't give a damn

Dessert?

Tragic tale

From 1848 onwards, about 40 expeditions searched for Sir Franklin, mapping the Canadian Arctic in the process. They learned from a note and Inuit accounts that Franklin's ships had been trapped and then crushed by ice. All the men eventually died of starvation and sickness trying to escape overland.

He went that-a-way

Sailor's goal

Although the northwest passage was of no practical use, completing it had now become a goal for explorers. It was finally sailed through in 1903–06 by Norwegian explorer Roald Amundsen, in a converted herring boat, *Gjoa*. His success was due to his use of Inuit survival methods.

Cold, cold heart

LOST NOT FOUND

To the Pacific Ocean

ARCTIC OCEAN

we're there!

GREENLAND

NORTH AMERICA

NORWAY

ICELAND

BRITAIN

EUROPE

HUDSON BAY

ATLANTIC OCEAN

— Martin Frobisher (1576)
— Henry Hudson (1610–11)
— Sir John Franklin (1845–47)
— Roald Amundsen (1903–06)

33

CROSSING NORTH AMERICA

From the 16th century, the North American continent was explored in the south by the Spanish, and in the north and west by the British and French. The Spanish were looking for gold, but found only hostile regions of deserts and mountains. Meanwhile, the British and French were searching for a waterway to the Pacific Ocean. Instead, they encountered a fertile land of rivers and lakes, rich in beaver and salmon, but home to fierce grizzly bears.

Seven cities of gold

In Mexico, the Spanish heard rumours of seven rich cities of gold somewhere in North America. In 1540, Francisco de Coronado headed a large expedition in search of these cities. He reached the Great Plains, and saw herds of buffalo (bison), but found no gold.

Bark canoes

French and British explorers travelled in Indian canoes built from birch bark. These were easy to repair and light enough to be carried overland from river to river.

Samuel de Champlain

The greatest French explorer was Samuel de Champlain, who founded the settlement of Quebec on the St Lawrence River in 1608. He was the first European to explore the Great Lakes, from 1609 onwards. One of these was later named Lake Champlain, in his honour.

Swamped in Florida

In 1539, Spanish explorer Hernando de Soto crossed into America from Cuba with an army of 622 men. He struggled though the Florida swamps and fought battles with native Americans in pursuit of gold. When he reached the Mississippi, he died of fever. There was no gold to be found.

Louisiana

Another Frenchman, Robert de la Salle, travelled south from the Great Lakes in 1682. He followed the great Mississippi River all the way to the Gulf of Mexico, and claimed the whole Mississippi region for France, naming it Louisiana after King Louis XIV.

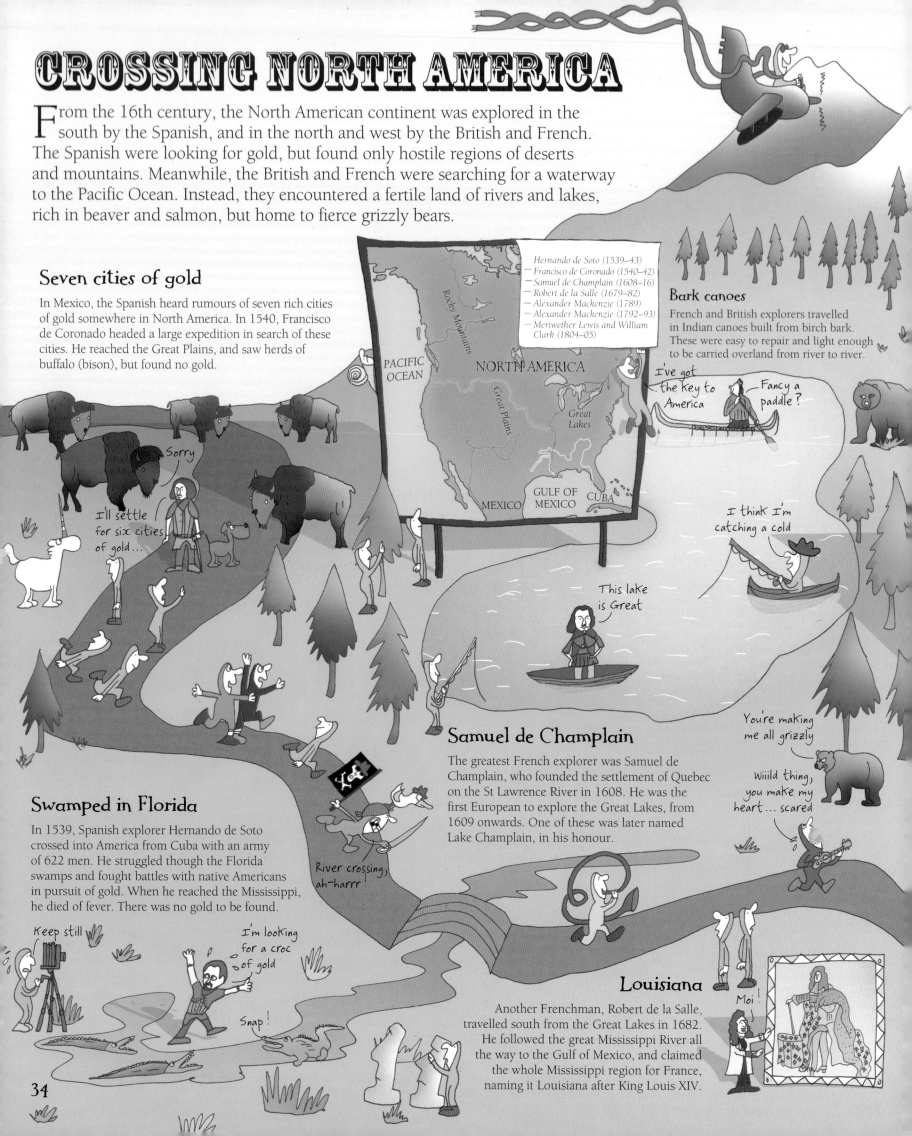

Hernando de Soto (1539–43)
Francisco de Coronado (1540–42)
Samuel de Champlain (1608–16)
Robert de la Salle (1679–82)
Alexander Mackenzie (1789)
Alexander Mackenzie (1792–93)
Meriwether Lewis and William Clark (1804–05)

PACIFIC OCEAN

NORTH AMERICA

Rocky Mountains

Great Plains

Great Lakes

MEXICO

GULF OF MEXICO

CUBA

I've got the key to America

Fancy a paddle?

I think I'm catching a cold

This lake is Great

You're making me all grizzly

Wiiild thing, you make my heart... scared

Sorry

I'll settle for six cities of gold...

River crossing, ah-harrr.

Keep still

I'm looking for a croc of gold

Snap!

Moi!

34

Over the Rockies

Alexander Mackenzie reached the Pacific Ocean on his second attempt in 1793 by following a series of rivers. This made him the first white man to cross America north of Mexico. He had to traverse the snowy Rocky Mountains, which formed a great barrier, blocking travel to the coast.

Snowshoes

Explorers learned from native American guides how to live and travel in the wild. They adopted the locals' webbed snowshoes made of wood and leather, which stopped them sinking into the soft snow.

Lewis and Clarke

In 1776, Britain's American colonies became the new United States of America. In 1804, US President Thomas Jefferson sent two explorers, called Meriwether Lewis and William Clark, on an expedition to follow the course of the great Missouri River. He hoped it would lead to the Pacific.

Fur traders

The northern lakes and rivers were rich in beaver. The soft, dense, and waterproof fur was prized in Europe, where it was made into hats. Canadian exploration was mostly carried out by two rival fur-trading companies, the Hudson's Bay Company and the Northwest Company.

River of Disappointment

The Scottish fur trader Alexander Mackenzie traced the course of a great western Canadian river in 1789, hoping it led to the Pacific Ocean. When he found that it took him north to the Arctic, he named it the "River of Disappointment". It was later called the Mackenzie River.

Native helper

After crossing the Rocky Mountains, Lewis and Clark reached the Pacific Ocean in November 1805. They were guided by a native American woman called Sacajawea, who had a baby on the journey.

Hunting

Native American hunters supplied the explorers with food, including deer and salmon. They fished with spears and basket traps, and shot deer and bear using guns, supplied by the fur traders.

Charting the Pacific

The greatest Pacific explorers were the Ancient Polynesians, whose ancestors came from Southeast Asia. They travelled around the Pacific Ocean looking for new island homes. By the 11th century CE, they had settled a vast area, from Hawaii in the north, to New Zealand in the southwest, and Easter Island in the southeast. When European explorers discovered their widely scattered islands in the 18th century, they were amazed to find them inhabited by a single people.

Routes taken by Polynesians

ASIA
NORTH AMERICA
PACIFIC OCEAN
HAWAIIAN ISLANDS
AUSTRALIA
NEW ZEALAND
EASTER ISLAND

We're making an exhibition of ourselves

Great voyages

At a time when European ships rarely sailed out of sight of land, Polynesians were making voyages in open sea of up to 4,800 km (3,000 miles). They sailed in large open-decked canoes, about 30 m (98 ft) in length, with twin hulls tied side by side. They navigated using the position of the Sun and stars.

Beginners welcome

ART STUDIO

I come from a land down under

Polynesian planning

Voyages were carefully planned to find new islands to settle. One double canoe could carry about 50 people, along with pigs, chickens, and dogs. They also brought many different plant seedlings, such as sweet potatoes and breadfruit. Rats travelled with them as well, either as stowaways on board or as emergency food supplies.

Copy my sense of perspective

I prefer a more abstract approach

Get my best angle

Art boars me

No use crying over spilled paint

I've drawn a blank

I'm world-renowned

Unknown continent

During the 18th century, Europeans searched the Pacific for a southern continent. Since the time of the Ancient Greeks, people had imagined that a land existed to balance the continents of the northern half of the globe. On maps, it was shown as "Terra Australis Incognita" (Unknown Southern land).

It's all going to pot

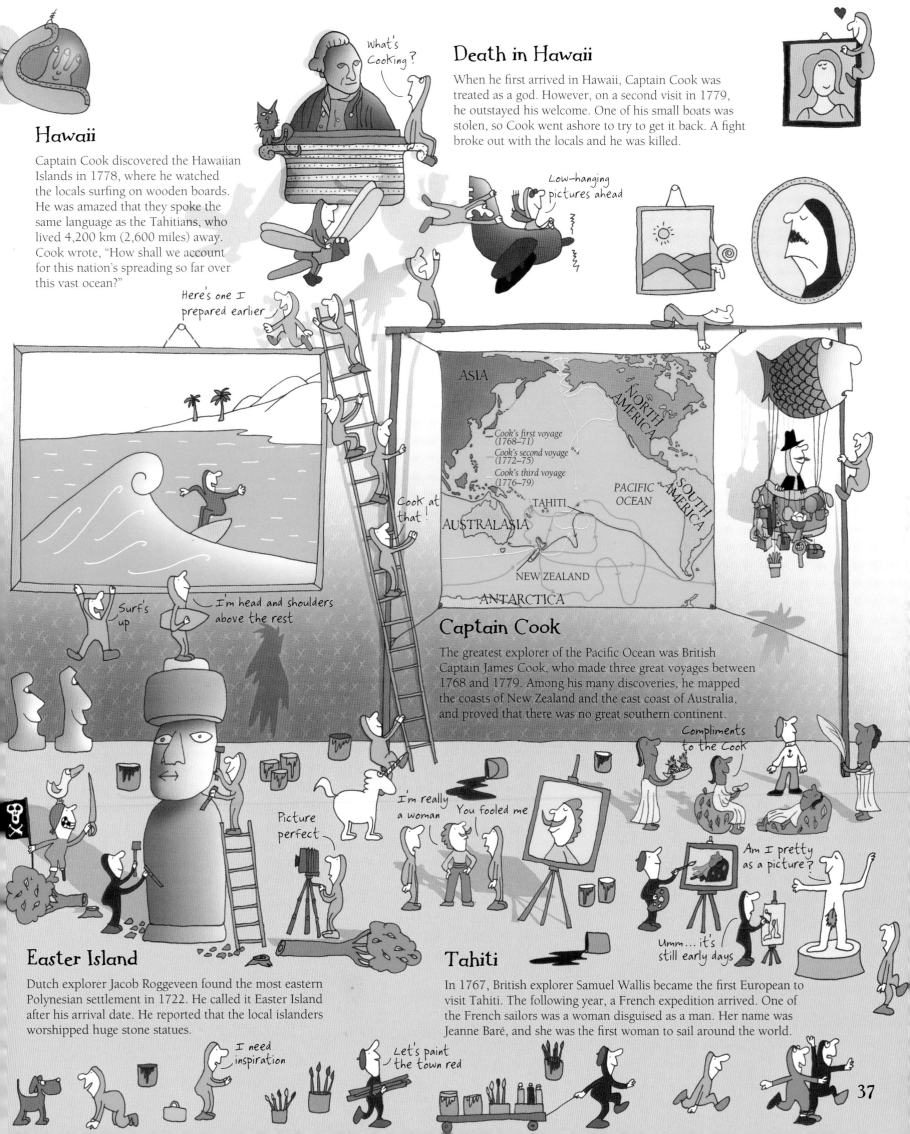

Hawaii

Captain Cook discovered the Hawaiian Islands in 1778, where he watched the locals surfing on wooden boards. He was amazed that they spoke the same language as the Tahitians, who lived 4,200 km (2,600 miles) away. Cook wrote, "How shall we account for this nation's spreading so far over this vast ocean?"

Death in Hawaii

When he first arrived in Hawaii, Captain Cook was treated as a god. However, on a second visit in 1779, he outstayed his welcome. One of his small boats was stolen, so Cook went ashore to try to get it back. A fight broke out with the locals and he was killed.

Captain Cook

The greatest explorer of the Pacific Ocean was British Captain James Cook, who made three great voyages between 1768 and 1779. Among his many discoveries, he mapped the coasts of New Zealand and the east coast of Australia, and proved that there was no great southern continent.

Easter Island

Dutch explorer Jacob Roggeveen found the most eastern Polynesian settlement in 1722. He called it Easter Island after his arrival date. He reported that the local islanders worshipped huge stone statues.

Tahiti

In 1767, British explorer Samuel Wallis became the first European to visit Tahiti. The following year, a French expedition arrived. One of the French sailors was a woman disguised as a man. Her name was Jeanne Baré, and she was the first woman to sail around the world.

Kangaroo

After sailing northwards, Cook spent seven weeks on the coast, repairing his ship. This gave Banks time to study the strange wildlife. He was baffled at the sight of "An animal as large as a greyhound, of a mouse colour and very swift". Aborigines told him it was called a kangaroo.

Flinders

In 1801, Lieutenant Matthew Flinders, a British naval officer, led the first expedition to sail all the way around Australia, on board *HMS Investigator*. Flinders mapped the whole coastline, and also suggested the name Australia, from "Terra Australis" (Southern land), for the area. His map showed the interior as a blank space.

Hop it!

Banksia serrata was a plant first collected and named by Banks

It's a blooming great place

It's blankety Banks

I'm an Austr-alien

Botany Bay

Captain James Cook landed on the east coast of Australia in 1770 and claimed the land for Britain. He named it New South Wales. His naturalist Joseph Banks collected so many previously unknown plants that Cook decided to call his landing place Botany Bay.

Terra Australis

The first explorers of Australia were the aborigines, whose ancestors made the earliest known sea voyages there from Asia more than 50,000 years ago. They learned how to live in a hot, dry landscape, finding water and food in unlikely places. European explorers began arriving from the 17th century, followed in the next century by settlers. They often looked down on aborigines, who had few clothes or possessions, but the aborigines were much better at surviving in the Australian "outback" (interior).

Tasman

The north coast of Australia was mapped in 1644 by Abel Tasman, a Dutch explorer. He was not impressed by Australia – then called New Holland – finding "Nothing profitable, only poor naked people". On an earlier voyage in 1642–43, Tasman discovered New Zealand and Tasmania, which was later named after him.

Dreamtime painting

Aborigines believe that they share their land with spirit beings, who live in a parallel world they call the "dreamtime". They paint pictures of the spirit beings on rocks, decorating them with coloured dots and circles.

That's the spirits!

New Zealand

Tasmania

What a devil

Settlers

The British founded a prison settlement on the east coast in 1788. Prisoners were soon followed by free settlers, who brought sheep and cattle with them, and who farmed along the coasts. Towns developed in the 19th century, including Sydney, Melbourne, and Adelaide. These became bases to explore the interior.

Inland sea?

The rivers of Southeast Australia flowed inland from mountains. This led to the hope that they might lead to an inland sea or fertile lake region. In 1828–30, the English explorer Charles Sturt traced the course of these rivers. He was disappointed to find that they only led south again, to the coast.

Going north

The most successful explorer of Australia was Scotsman John McDouall Stuart. He realized that the only way to travel was light and fast. Three of his six expeditions set off from Adelaide in southern Australia, and one of these became the first south-to-north crossing of the continent in 1861–62. His route was later used to lay a telegraph line.

Disaster

In 1860, Robert O'Hara Burke led a big expedition, with 24 camels and 23 horses, from Melbourne to the north coast. Unlike Stuart, he knew nothing of the outback. On the return journey, Burke and two companions starved to death. A fourth man, John King, was saved by aborigines, who nursed him until searchers arrived.

Surviving the south

In 1840–41, Englishman Edward Eyre explored the south coast to the west of Adelaide, with an aborigine friend called Wylie. They hoped to find grazing land, but found only waterless desert. They survived by collecting dew from bushes, until they were eventually rescued by a French whaling ship.

Trapped by a creek

Still hoping to find an inland sea, Charles Sturt set off with a large expedition in 1844. This included 15 men, 11 horses, 30 bullocks, 200 sheep, and a boat. Instead of a sea, he found a scorching desert. He was trapped for seven months beside a sinking creek, until rains finally came.

INTO AFRICA

Although Europeans had known about Africa for thousands of years, it was one of the last continents they explored. The risks were great and the rewards seemed few. In the north, there was the challenging Sahara Desert, while to the south, there were dangerous animals, hostile tribes, and tropical diseases. Despite this, from the late 18th century, a few brave explorers set off for the "White Man's Grave", as Africa was known.

Timbuktu triumph

Another Scotsman, named Alexander Gordon Laing, crossed the Sahara Desert in 1825. He narrowly survived an attack by Tuareg tribesmen, reaching Timbuktu in August 1826. However, as he was leaving, he was murdered.

Search for Timbuktu

One goal of exploration was to find a glorious West African city called Timbuktu, mentioned by medieval Muslim travellers. It was said to be so wealthy that its houses were roofed with gold.

Travelling in disguise

In 1824, the French Geographical Society offered a big cash prize to the first European to reach Timbuktu and return alive. René Caillié, who spoke Arabic, decided to go there disguised as an Egyptian Muslim.

Big disappointment

René Caillié arrived in Timbuktu in April 1828. He was disappointed by the city, which he described as "A mass of ill-looking houses built of earth". Back home, he won the prize, but his health never recovered.

Rocky rapids

On a second Niger journey in 1805, Park hoped to avoid trouble by staying in a boat. However in April 1806, his boat got stuck on a rock while travelling down some rapids. Attacked by tribesmen, Park jumped overboard and drowned.

Daylight robbery

Among other hardships, Mungo Park fell sick, and was imprisoned for four months by a Muslim ruler. Worst of all, Park was robbed in August 1796, in the middle of the rainy season. Thieves took his horse, belongings, and clothes.

James Bruce

In 1768, a Scottish explorer named James Bruce sailed to Africa to find the source of the Nile River. This problem had baffled people for thousands of years. He was welcomed at the royal court of Ethiopia, where he stayed for two years.

Blue Nile

James Bruce reached the source of the Blue Nile in 1770, believing he had solved the mystery of the great river. However, although the Blue Nile flows into the Nile, it is not its main source, which is much further south.

African Association

A dozen wealthy Britons got together in 1788 to establish the African Association. This was set up to fund exploration of the country's interior. One of their first projects was to find the Niger, a great river somewhere in West Africa, described by medieval Muslim travellers.

Mungo Park

In 1795, the African Association sent a young Scotsman, called Mungo Park, to West Africa to find the Niger River. After many adventures, Park became the first European to see the river, and discovered that it flowed from east to west.

EUROPE

ASIA

Alexandria

Sahara Desert

AFRICA

Timbuktu

ETHIOPIA

— James Bruce's route (1768–71)
— Mungo Park's first route (1795–97)
— Mungo Park's second route (1805–06)
— Alexander Gordon Laing's route (1825–26)
— René Caillié's route (1827–28)

ATLANTIC
OCEAN

Burton and Speke

Europeans heard stories of a region of great lakes in East Africa. In 1857, two British explorers, Richard Burton and John Hanning Speke, set off to find them. Early in 1858 they reached a lake the locals called Tanganyika. Speke, who was temporarily blind, could not see its glittering waters.

Meeting

David Livingstone returned to Africa in 1866. No one heard from him for more than two years, and in 1868 the Welsh-born US journalist Henry Morton Stanley was sent by his newspaper to find the explorer. He tracked him down in 1871, greeting him with the words, "Dr Livingstone, I presume?"

Victoria Falls

While following the Zambesi River in 1855, David Livingstone reached a mighty waterfall that the local people called "The smoke that thunders". Livingstone renamed it Victoria Falls, after his queen. In 1864, he returned to Britain, where he was given a hero's welcome. Despite this, he was anxious to get back to Africa.

Lion attack

David Livingstone was attacked by a lion in 1844, which grabbed him by the shoulder. He wrote, "Growling horribly close to my ear, he shook me as a terrier dog does a rat". Luckily, the lion dropped Livingstone and he recovered, though his left arm was permanently disabled.

Victorians in Africa

Between the 1840s and 1870s, Victorian explorers were facing the challenges of Africa in order to map the continent's interior. They traced the Zambezi and Congo Rivers, and found a region of lakes in East Africa. Africans couldn't understand the motivations of these explorers. In 1863, an African chief called Kamurasi met British explorer Samuel Baker, who said he was searching for a lake. Kamurasi declared, "No man would leave his own country and people, and face danger and fatigue, merely to look at water!"

Livingstone's life

The Scottish missionary David Livingstone first travelled to Africa in 1841. Hoping to end the slave trade, he spent his life exploring the land. For 32 years, he travelled 64,000 km (40,000 miles), mostly on foot and with only a few African companions.

ATLANTIC OCEAN

ASIA

AFRICA

Lake Albert

Lake Victoria

Victoria Falls

— David Livingstone (1841)
— David Livingstone (1849–56)
— Richard Burton and John Speke (1857–58)
— John Speke (1858)
— David Livingstone (1858–64)
— John Speke (1860–63)
— Samuel and Florence Baker (1861–65)
— David Livingstone (1866–73)
— Henry Morton Stanley (1874–77)
— Henry Morton Stanley (1887–89)

Lake Victoria

Richard Burton then fell sick and was unable to travel. On a solo mission, Speke headed north to another great lake, which he called Lake Victoria, after the queen. He was sure that this was the source of the Nile River. Burton thought Speke was wrong and they became bitter enemies.

Source of the Nile

In 1860, Speke returned to explore Lake Victoria, and found the Nile River flowing out of its north end. He went home, planning to confront Burton with this evidence in a public debate. On the day of the meeting, Speke shot himself, perhaps by accident, while hunting.

Married mission

During the 1860s, Samuel and Florence Baker, a husband and wife team, were also looking for the sources of the Nile. In 1864, they found another great lake, north of Victoria, with waters also flowing into the Nile. They named this Lake Albert, after Queen Victoria's husband.

Congo expedition

After finding Livingstone, Henry Morton Stanley became an African explorer in his own right. From 1876, he traced the entire course of the Congo River. While Livingstone travelled light, Stanley had an army of 350 African porters, carrying supplies including a portable steamboat.

Congo battles

The African tribes who lived by the Congo River saw the arrival of Stanley's huge expedition as an invasion. As a result, Stanley had to fight 32 fierce battles along the river, losing more than half his men. By tracing the Congo River, Stanley had solved the last great mystery of African exploration.

43

Scientist explorers

The desire for scientific knowledge became a powerful new motive for exploration by the late 18th century. Scientist explorers travelled to remote lands, where they identified previously unknown plant and animal species. They brought back specimens for museums and gardens, and made amazing discoveries about the workings of the natural world.

Humboldt

In 1799, the German scientist Alexander von Humboldt spent five years exploring 9,600 km (6,000 miles) of northwest South America. With companion Aimé Bonpland, he collected plant and animal specimens, and studied geology, ocean currents, weather patterns, and the magnetism of Earth.

Recorded findings

On returning to Europe, Humboldt spent 20 years publishing the results of his expedition in 34 huge illustrated volumes. These writings inspired younger naturalists, including Charles Darwin, who described Humboldt as "The greatest scientific traveller who ever lived".

Darwin

In 1831, the British naturalist Charles Darwin set sail on a naval survey ship, *HMS Beagle*. For five years, Darwin travelled the coast of South America and explored the Galapagos Islands. He found the island birds, though related to South American ones, were different species.

Finches

In the Galapagos Islands, Darwin discovered 13 species of finch, each with different shaped beaks, adapted for the food available on its island. Darwin concluded that they had all descended from the same species of South American finch, but they had evolved into different species.

Natural selection

Darwin realized that, within a species, individual animals vary slightly from each other. Those born with features better suited to their environment are more likely to survive to have offspring. Their features will be passed on to their young. As small changes build up, new species appear in a process he called "natural selection".

The Origin of Species

Although Darwin came up with his theory in 1838, he did not publish it until 1859, after learning that a fellow British naturalist, Alfred Russell Wallace, had come up with the same idea. Darwin's book *The Origin of Species* was an instant bestseller.

SOUTH AMERICA

GALAPAGOS ISLANDS

P-p-pick up a penguin

Do I know you?

One of my feathered friends

Surely my bag will come out soon?

Who is the book worm?

Is this terminal two?

Slippery sucker

A little light reading

Wish I could evolve some wheels

You'd look good in my living room

You've got a lot of bottle

Sign here, please

It's rude to stare

Wonder where we're going

Wallace in South America

Travelling along South America's Amazon River in 1848–52, Alfred Russell Wallace gathered insects, which he planned to sell to museums on his return. During the journey home, his ship caught fire. Wallace lived, but his collection and most of his notes were destroyed.

SOUTH AMERICA

Bates

Wallace's companion, Henry Bates, stayed behind in South America for more than a decade, collecting 14,000 specimens, including 8,000 previously unknown insects. To avoid Wallace's fate, Bates sent his collection home on three different ships. In 1863, he published a book describing his travels, *The Naturalist on the River Amazons*.

LOST LUGGAGE

Wallace in Malaya

In 1854, Wallace travelled to Malaya, where he spent the next eight years building up a new collection of more than 125,000 specimens, with 80,000 of them beetles. By studying his insects, Wallace, like Charles Darwin, realized that all living species have evolved by natural selection.

The Wallace Line

Wallace found that the animals and plants of western and eastern Malaya were different. The reason was that the eastern ones were of Australian origin, while the western ones came from Asia. The boundary between the two regions is known as the Wallace Line.

WEST MALAYA

EAST MALAYA

NORTH POLE

A major challenge for explorers in the 19th century was reaching the treacherous North Pole. This is the most northerly point on the planet, sitting in the middle of a vast frozen sea, called the Arctic Ocean. Like other seas, the Arctic has powerful currents, which make the ice sheets move, so it is very difficult to travel there.

Sledging backwards

A British naval officer named William Parry tried to reach the North Pole by sledge in 1827. Setting off from the Norwegian island of Spitzbergen, he gave up after discovering that the ice sheets were moving south faster than he could travel north.

Frozen in

The Norwegian Fridtjof Nansen was a man with a plan in 1893. He allowed his strengthened ship, *Fram*, to be frozen into the ice, hoping that the Arctic currents would carry him to the North Pole. *Fram* spent three years in the ice, but drifted south of Nansen's goal.

Lost toes

In the early 1900s, US explorer Robert Peary tried eight times to get to the North Pole. On the first attempt, he lost eight toes to frostbite. Peary told his shocked travelling companion, Matthew Henson, "A few toes aren't much to achieve the Pole!"

Pole rivalry

In 1909, Robert Peary and a rival US explorer, Frederick Cook, each claimed to have reached the North Pole. At the time, people believed Peary and not Cook. However, modern experts argue that Peary could not have reached the North Pole in the time available.

Further conquests

Although no one knows for sure who got to the North Pole first, it has been visited several times since Robert Peary's day by airship, aircraft, and even submarine. The first certain land crossing was made in 1968 by US explorer Ralph Plaisted, who travelled in a snowmobile.

SOUTH POLE

To reach the South Pole, explorers had to cross icy Antarctica, the coldest and windiest place on Earth. Another problem was that the Pole sits on a high plateau, about 3,000 m (9,800 ft) above sea level. Though it is the fifth largest continent, Antarctica is so far from inhabited land that it was only discovered in the 13th century.

Ice ice baby

The southern continent

The existence of an Antarctic continent was discovered by Captain James Cook, who sailed around it from 1772. Although he did not see the continent itself, he knew it must be there from the many icebergs, which only form on land.

This is a snow go area

Freeze frame

To the South Pole

The first attempt to reach the South Pole was by British explorer, Robert Falcon Scott, in 1902–03. He gave up when a companion, Ernest Shackleton, fell ill with scurvy. Leading a second expedition in 1908, Shackleton got within 770 km (480 miles) of the Pole.

So near ... and yet so far

This place gives me the chills

Race to the Pole

By 1910, the quest for the South Pole had become a race between a Norwegian expedition, led by Roald Amundsen, and another British expedition, headed by Robert Falcon Scott. Using expert skiers and dog sledges, Amundsen won, reaching the Pole on 12 December 1911.

Down and out

Scott's team dragged their sledge to the Pole, making the journey much harder. They arrived on 17 January 1912 to find the Norwegian flag already flying. They died on the return journey, weakened by frostbite, scurvy, and exhaustion.

I'm dog tired

Pipped at the Pole

Oh, snow!

I've been left out in the cold

Ross Ice Shelf

In 1838, James Clark Ross led a British naval expedition, mapping much of the Antarctic coastline. Over five years, he discovered two volcanoes and an ice shelf the size of France joined onto the continent. This was later named the Ross Ice Shelf in his honour.

Antarctica leaves me cold

Very ice, too

SOUTH AMERICA

PACIFIC OCEAN

ROSS SEA

ANTARCTICA

• South Pole

Ross Ice Shelf

NEW ZEALAND

AUSTRALIA

INDIAN OCEAN

— James Clark Ross (1838–41)
— James Clark Ross (1841–43)
— Roald Amundsen (1910–11)
— Robert Falcon Scott (1910–12)

Ocean depths

Although deep oceans cover most of Earth's surface, little was known about them until the 19th century. People believed that the deep sea was too cold and the water pressure too great for anything to live there. With the 1872 voyage of the British research ship, *HMS Challenger*, a new science, called oceanography, was born. During a four-year voyage of exploration, *HMS Challenger* found mountains, trenches, and a seabed teeming with life.

HMS Challenger

This British naval warship was converted into a floating laboratory. Equipped with bottles for sea water samples, weighted ropes for measuring depths, and dredging nets for scooping up sea life, *HMS Challenger*'s mission was "To find out everything about the sea".

New species

HMS Challenger was a success story, finding 4,717 previously unknown species of marine life. New discoveries included fish with huge eyes and fish able to create their own light, both adaptations to help them live in the dark depths.

Sound mapping

From the late 1940s, the ocean floors were mapped using sonar. This technology works by sending sound waves down from a surface ship and recording the echo sent back. Using sonar, oceanographers mapped the world's ridges and trenches, and discovered that they matched areas where earthquakes and volcanoes were common.

Bathysphere

The US inventor and diver, Frederick Otis Barton, created a craft for exploring the sea in 1928. Called the bathysphere, it was lowered from a ship on a cable and carried a crew of two. The bathysphere made its first descent into the ocean in 1930.

I'm going to li-lo

Hook, line, and sinker

Name that tuna?

Just in time for the seafood special

I won't take the bait

Super sound effects

Some bunny help me

All going swimmingly

You look out of plaice

Back off, fish face

48

Hydrothermal vents

In the 1970s, the US manned submersible, Alvin, explored hydrothermal vents – hot springs on the ocean floor where mineral-rich fluids flow from Earth's crust. Even here, many new creatures were found, including strange fish, crabs, and shrimps.

Tube worms

One of the most bizarre creatures found living by the hydrothermal vents was the tube worm, which grows up to 2.4 m (8 ft) in length.

Tube worm

Undersea mountains

In the middle of the Atlantic Ocean, HMS Challenger discovered a large ridge, running from the Arctic to the South Atlantic. Called the Mid-Atlantic Ridge, this is the longest mountain chain on Earth.

Seismic exploration

Today, geologists probe the ocean floor using seismic exploration. This involves setting off explosions or transmitting vibrations from ships. Shock waves travel underground, and are then reflected back by different materials beneath the seabed. The method, invented in the 1930s for use on land, is now used to find undersea oil and gas deposits.

Surface ship

Signal is transmitted from the ship

Sound detectors, towed behind the ship, pick up the echoes

SEISMIC EXPLORATION

Bathyscaphe

Following on from the bathysphere was the bathyscaphe of the 1940s. A Swiss scientist named Auguste Piccard invented this new deep-sea diving submarine. Unlike the bathysphere, the bathyscaphe did not need to be tethered to a surface vessel, so there was huge opportunity for underwater exploration.

Changing Earth

Studies of the seabed reveal that Earth's surface is made up of about a dozen great plates, positioned on top of molten rock. Ridges form when plates move apart and molten rock flows up, forming new land, while, at the trenches, one plate is pushed beneath another.

Trieste

In 1960, Auguste Piccard's son, Jacques, took the bathyscaphe Trieste down 10,916 m (35,814 ft) to the bottom of the Pacific's Marianas Trench, the deepest point in the ocean. It took Piccard and crew member Don Walsh more than three hours to return to the surface.

Arggh! Monster of the deep

I've got bigger fish to fry

I've earned my water wings

Is that a flying fish?

Shoal us the way

Cod on then

Cracks are starting to show

That's deep, maaan

Given to me on a plate

I'm at my lowest point

MOUNTAIN PEAKS

In the 18th century, Europeans began to embrace the challenge of climbing mountains. Initially, climbers were scientists, who wanted to carry out research. Later, people were driven by the desire to be the first to climb particular peaks. Mountaineers started by climbing the Alps of Europe. Once these mountains had all been conquered, they turned to the Himalayas of Asia, a range that includes Everest, the world's highest mountain. When English mountaineer George Mallory was asked why he wanted to climb Everest, he replied, "Because it's there!"

Blanc blindness

The highest mountain in the Alps is Mont Blanc, which rises 4,810 m (15,780 ft) above sea level. It was first climbed in 1786 by a French doctor named Michel-Gabriel Paccard, with his guide, Jacques Balmat. Dazzled by the bright snow, both men went temporarily blind during the climb.

Measuring the mountain

Paccard climbed Mont Blanc for scientific reasons. He wanted to work out the mountain's height using a barometer – an instrument for measuring air pressure. Paccard hoped to prove that it was the tallest mountain in Europe. Unfortunately, when he got to the top, he found that his barometer was broken!

Climbing for sport

During the 1850s, British tourists on holiday in the Alps began climbing them for sport. The fashion started in 1854, when a young English lawyer named Alfred Wills climbed the 3,692-m- (12,112-ft-) high Wetterhorn. Wills celebrated by planting a fir tree at the top. Over the next ten years, 50 more alpine peaks were conquered.

Basic equipment

Victorian climbers had only basic mountaineering equipment. This included ropes to tie themselves together, ice axes to cut steps in the snow, and long walking sticks with metal spikes, called alpenstocks. They dressed in the same heavy tweed clothes they might wear for a walk in the countryside.

Hundreds and thousands, millions and billions!

Beautiful blizzard ahead

More the merrier

The sweet taste of victory

Dream team

On top of the world

In 1953, the New Zealander Edmund Hillary and Sherpa Tenzing Norgay took part in an English expedition to conquer Everest. On 29 May, the two climbers reached the summit, where they hugged each other with joy. Tenzing buried sweets at the top, as an offering to the mountain.

Enough of your sweet-talk

It must be love

Matterhorn mishap

The deadliest mountain in the Alps is the Matterhorn. It was first climbed in 1865 by the English mountaineer Edward Whymper, with six other men. Coming back down, one climber slipped and fell off the slope, pulling three others to their deaths. Whymper and two guides survived only because the rope attaching them to the others snapped.

Sherpa guides

Mountaineers in the Himalayas hired the local people, called Sherpas, to be guides and porters. With lungs suited to the thin air, Sherpas are excellent climbers. They see Mount Everest as a holy place and call it *Chomolungma* ("Goddess Mother of the World").

River deep, mountain highhhh

Does it really Matter?

I don't know whether to climb it or eat it

Like this?

Smile, please

Yodelayheehoo

Frozen in time

In the 1920s, English climber George Mallory took part in three Everest expeditions. On the last, in 1924, he disappeared close to the summit, along with his companion, Andrew Irvine. It was not until 1999 that Mallory's frozen body was found on the mountain. No one knows whether he reached the top before he died.

Bleat it

That's cheating

You make it look so easy

I'd see a dentist about that...

So I'm the cat that got the cream

I'm going round the bend

Himalayan heights

The tallest mountains on Earth are the Himalayas, situated between India and China. Highest of all is Mount Everest, reaching 8,848 m (29,028 ft) above sea level. Climbing is made difficult by the strong winds, freezing cold, and reduced oxygen in the air. From 1924, climbers used bottled oxygen to help them breathe at altitude.

Back to base for me

Fallen heroes

Many mountaineers did not reach the Matterhorn's summit of 4,504 m (14,780 ft). The difficulty of climbing the sheer faces and battling frequent falls of rock and snow caused many casualties. Since 1865, more than 500 climbers have been killed trying to climb the mountain.

Happy campers

51

Chinese in Space

By the 1990s, China had joined the Space race, launching a series of spacecraft. The first manned mission was Shenzhou 5, in 2003. Astronaut Yang Liwei made a 21-hour flight, completing 14 orbits of Earth. On his return, he was awarded the title of "Space Hero".

Shenzhou's re-entry capsule could seat three crew members

Hubble telescope

In 1990, the US launched a Space telescope called Hubble. Orbiting outside Earth's atmosphere, which distorts and blocks light, Hubble has a much clearer view of Space than telescopes on Earth. It has sent back hundreds of thousands of pictures of distant parts of the Universe.

Hubble is about the same size as a school bus

So-viet near yet So-viet far!

Space probes

Unmanned craft, commonly called Space probes, are sent into Space to take photographs of parts of our Solar System. Probes have now been launched by the USA, Russia, China, the European Union, Japan, and India. They have photographed the other planets, their moons, comets, and asteroids.

SpaceShipOne

The first privately funded spacecraft was SpaceShipOne, a rocket-powered plane funded by US multimillionaire Paul Allen. In 2004, US pilot Mike Melvill became the first commercial astronaut on SpaceShipOne. Several companies are now developing spacecraft to fly private citizens to Space.

SpaceShipOne offers passengers six minutes of weightlessness on an edge-of-Space trip

JUN 2004

International Space Station

The 1990s saw the start of a new era of international co-operation in Space exploration. The USA, Russia, Japan, Canada, and the European Union joined together to build the International Space Station, which began construction in 1998. This Space laboratory orbits Earth, and is continually manned by astronauts.

The ISS consists of 18 major parts, which were launched separately and assembled in Space

NOV 1998

I'm over the Moon!

We've won!

One small step

While Collins stayed on board the command module, Armstrong and Aldrin took the landing module down to the Moon, where they landed safely on 20 July. As he stepped onto the lunar surface, Armstrong famously said, "That's one small step for (a) man, one giant leap for mankind". The US had won the Space race by landing men on the Moon.

When the Moon hits your eye like a big pizza pie, that's... painful

Moon mission

On 16 July 1969, about 600 million people around the world watched the live television broadcast of the launch of Apollo 11, the US Moon mission. The craft carried three astronauts, Neil Armstrong, Edwin "Buzz" Aldrin, and Michael Collins. After three days in Space, the astronauts reached the Moon.

JUL 1969

Apollo 11's rocket guzzled 13,000 litres (3,500 gallons) of fuel every second

INTO SPACE

The world's two most powerful nations, the USA and the Soviet Union (USSR), began a race to explore Space in the 1950s. Each superpower saw winning the race as a matter of national pride, but also feared that the other might launch deadly weapons from Space. It became the most expensive programme of exploration in history, and its greatest achievement came in 1969, when the USA landed the first men on the Moon. Several other countries, and even private companies, have begun to explore Space since.

US Space programmes

From 1962, NASA organized three big Space programmes. The Mercury programme put the first American, John Glenn, into orbit that year. By 1964, the Gemini programme was developing new methods for Space travel, sending astronauts on longer flights. The Apollo programme, from 1966–75, carried men to the Moon.

NASA

The USA started their own Space programme in 1958, run by the National Aeronautics and Space Administration (NASA). Its chief designer was a German, Wernher von Braun. Like Korolev, he had developed rockets as weapons in World War II.

USSR

The Soviet Space programme was headed by the brilliant scientist Sergei Korolev, who had designed rocket weapons in World War II. His work was so secret that his identity was not revealed until 1990, 24 years after his death. In his lifetime, he was known only as the "Chief Designer".

Sputnik 1

The Soviets raced out of the blocks in 1957, by launching the first man-made object into Space. This was a satellite of 58 cm (23 in) in diameter, called Sputnik 1. It orbited Earth, sending back radio signals for 22 days, before its batteries ran out.

Humans in Space

In the early days, the USSR seemed to be winning the Space race. In 1961, the Russian Yuri Gagarin became the first man to travel in Space, on Vostok 1. In 1963, Valentina Tereshkova became the first woman in Space on Vostok 6.

Ham

In 1961, the USA sent a chimp called Ham into Space. Ham successfully returned to Earth, suffering only a bruised nose.

Laika

Just a month after Sputnik 1, the USSR launched Sputnik 2, which was the first craft to carry a live passenger into orbit. This was a dog called Laika, who sadly died soon after take-off.

53

The future

We will continue to explore outer Space in the future, sending missions to the planets and moons of our Solar System, and perhaps even beyond. There is also much left to be discovered on Earth, where new living species continue to be identified.

2005
After a seven-year journey, the European Space Agency's Huygens probe lands on Titan, a moon of Saturn. This is the first landing on a moon other than Earth's.

1998
The Russians launch the first part of the International Space Station, a Space laboratory orbiting Earth. It is used for scientific experiments by astronauts from many nations.

1961
Soviet cosmonaut, Yuri Gagarin, is the first man in Space. Eight years later, the US astronauts Neil Armstrong and Edwin "Buzz" Aldrin become the first men on the Moon.

1960
Jacques Piccard and Don Walsh reach the deepest point on the ocean floor in the deep-sea diving vessel *Trieste*.

Keep goating!

1953
A big British expedition climbs Mount Everest, the world's tallest mountain. The peak is reached by a New Zealander, Edmund Hillary, and Tenzing Norgay, a Sherpa.

Modern explorers

By the middle of the 20th century, the whole world had been mapped, yet explorers found new tests. The world's highest mountain was scaled, the deepest point in the ocean floor was reached, and there was a race to explore Space.

1519
Ferdinand Magellan leads a Spanish fleet in the first crossing of the Pacific. He dies in the Philippines, but one ship completes the first voyage around the world.

Northern voyages

From the 16th century, the British and Dutch grew envious of the wealth of Spain and Portugal. They also tried to reach Asia, but by sailing northwest and northeast. However, explorers found only icy regions and many died on their search for the northern passages.

I should have brought a coat

1553
Sir Hugh Willoughby leads an English expedition in search of a northeast passage to Asia, but freezes to death off Lapland.

1596
The Dutch seafarer Willem Barents sails in search of the northeast passage. He discovers and names Spitzbergen ("Jagged Peaks"), and spends winter on the Arctic islands of Novaya Zemlya, but dies on his return journey.

Can we not be friends?

1610
English explorer Henry Hudson searches for a northwest passage. He sails into Hudson Bay, where his ship is trapped by ice. When the ice melts, his crew mutinies and abandons him.

Spice up my life

1498
Vasco da Gama, a Portuguese explorer, makes the first voyage from Europe to India, returning with a valuable cargo of spices. More than half his men die of scurvy.

Hi, chaps

1492
Christopher Columbus, an Italian serving Spain, sails across the Atlantic Ocean and reaches the Caribbean Islands in 1492. He founds Hispaniola, the first European settlement in the Americas, a year later.

1487
The Portuguese seafarer, Bartolomeu Dias, sails around the southern tip of Africa, making the first European voyage into the Indian Ocean. This opens a sea route to India.

I'll put my neck on the line

1405
China sends out the first of six expeditions commanded by Zheng He, who visits lands in the Indian Ocean. His fleets include the largest wooden ships ever built, and he returns with exotic wonders, including a giraffe.

The Great Age of Exploration

The period from the 15th to early 16th centuries was the greatest era in world exploration. It began with Chinese voyages to the southern seas. Later, Portuguese and Spanish expeditions sailed to India, discovered America, and sailed all the way around the world.

Trip through time

Throughout the ages, there have been various motives for exploration. The Viking Age saw sailors looking for new lands to settle. In the 15th century, Europeans sought a sea route to the wealth of Asia. Unravelling the mysteries of the Universe is the main reason for exploration in modern times. One successful expedition or breakthrough can inspire other explorers to set off, ensuring more new ground is broken in the future.

Prehistoric Age

Our ancestors were hunter-gatherers, who left Africa 70,000 years ago and set off in search of new lands to settle. At first, they stayed close to the warm tropics, moving east across Asia. Later, they found their way to Australia, Europe, and the Americas.

Water way to go

c.50,000 BCE
Australia is settled by people from Southeast Asia, who make the earliest known sea journey. They have to cross 90 km (56 miles) of open water to reach it.

Polar exploration

From the late 19th century, exploration became a question of facing great challenges. The greatest of all were reaching the North and South Poles, which are the most hostile places on Earth. Explorers raced to be first to the Poles and plant their country's flag there.

1911

A Norwegian expedition, led by Roald Amundsen, and a British one, led by Robert Falcon Scott, both race to the South Pole. Amundsen, using dog sledges, is the winner.

1909

After eight attempts, US explorer Robert Peary claims to have reached the North Pole. Given the short time he took, it is unlikely that his claim was true.

1872

HMS Challenger, a converted British Navy warship, sails around the world investigating the oceans. The expedition discovers undersea mountain ranges, and finds life in the deep ocean.

1862

Scottish explorer John McDouall Stuart completes the first south-to-north crossing of Australia. His route is later used for a telegraph line and a road, the Stuart Highway.

1857

In West Africa, the English explorers John Hanning Speke and Richard Burton reach a region of Great Lakes. Speke discovers that one lake is the source of the Nile River, and names it Lake Victoria after his queen.

Victorian explorers

During the Victorian Age, explorers traced rivers in Africa, and crossed the Australian interior. There was a new attempt to find a northwest passage. Though it was unsuccessful, the expeditions led to the mapping of the Canadian Arctic.

The Scientific Age

In the late 18th century, expeditions were driven by a new thirst for scientific knowledge. Explorers of the time travelled with scientific observers, such as botanists. New scientific research societies sent out expeditions to fill in the spaces on the maps.

1768

Captain James Cook, a British explorer, sets sail on the first of three great voyages of exploration in the Pacific. He charts the east coast of Australia, and discovers the Hawaiian Islands.

1796

A Scottish explorer called Mungo Park is the first European to see Africa's Niger River. He is sent by the African Association, a scientific body founded by wealthy Britons.

1799

The German scientist, Alexander von Humboldt, explores northwest South America, collecting data on geology, weather, butterflies, and plants. He inspires later scientific travellers, including Charles Darwin.

1324

Ibn Battuta, a Muslim scholar from Morocco, sets out on the first of many journeys in Asia, as well as East and West Africa. He travels at least 120,000 km (75,000 miles) during 30 years of travelling.

1271

The explorer Marco Polo of Italy travels east to China along the Silk Road. After 24 years of exploration, he describes the lands he has visited in a famous book.

c.980 CE

Erik the Red, a Norwegian settler in Iceland, explores and settles Greenland. About 20 years later, his son Leif Erikson reaches a region of North America he calls Vinland.

c.865 CE

A Norwegian Viking called Floki Raven explores and names Iceland, after spending a cold winter there. Soon, settlers from Norway arrive.

The Middle Ages

The greatest explorers of the early Middle Ages were the Vikings of Scandinavia, who sailed west across the North Sea and Atlantic Ocean, discovering and settling new lands. In the later Middle Ages, Europeans travelled east along the Silk Road, a trade route linking China with the Mediterranean world.

c.16,000 BCE

America is settled by hunters from Asia. They follow herds of animals over a land bridge between the two continents.

Ancient explorers

The earliest explorers we know by name were the Ancient Egyptians, Greeks, and Phoenicians. These were trading peoples, searching for goods such as metals and spices. After exploring the Mediterranean, they sailed north into the Atlantic, and south around Africa.

c.1470 BCE

Queen Hatshepsut of Egypt sends a fleet of ships on a trading mission to Punt, somewhere in East Africa. This is the first recorded expedition.

c.600 BCE

Phoenician explorers sail clockwise all the way around Africa for Pharaoh Necho II of Egypt. It takes almost three years to complete their journey.

c.310 BCE

The Greek explorer Pytheas sails around Britain and reaches a northern land he calls Thule. This is probably Iceland or Norway. He writes that the midsummer Sun does not set there.

Unknown future

A century ago, no one thought that people could travel to the Moon. In the same way, we cannot know exactly where explorers will travel in the future. Perhaps, one day, it may even be possible to travel through time, or to distant galaxies.

On to Mars

Another NASA plan is to send a rocket to Mars and back, bringing samples collected by robotic vehicles. Mars once had water, and may have had life. The aim is to learn if there was life on Mars in the past, and what happened to it.

Back to the Moon

As part of its new Constellation mission, NASA is building a fleet of rockets to return astronauts to the Moon, and hopefully allow them to spend long periods of time living there. Learning to live on the Moon is preparation for further Space exploration.

Tracking comets

The extinction of the dinosaurs, about 65 million years ago, was caused by a comet or asteroid hitting Earth. One practical reason for future Space exploration is to track comets and asteroids, and to deflect them if they are on course for our planet.

Life in Space

One goal of Space exploration is to see if there is life on other planets and moons. The most likely place to find life is on Europa, a moon of Jupiter, thought to have an ice-covered ocean. A joint European/NASA mission to Europa is planned for 2020.

Antarctic lake

One of the world's largest lakes was recently discovered beneath the ice sheets covering Antarctica. The water of Lake Vostok is one million years old. Russian scientists plan to send a robot probe, called a cryobot, into the lake to see if life exists there.

Heating its way through the ice, the cryobot takes measurements and collects data

Tree navigation

Rainforests are home to millions of unknown species of animals, plants, and insects. The hardest area to study is the canopy (top level) of the trees. Using a new technology called dendronautics (tree navigation), scientists can now study the canopy, travelling in small airships.

Super squids

The giant squid and colossal squid are two huge species that live in the deep ocean, where they are hunted by sperm whales. So far, only dead specimens have been found. It is hoped that one day these remarkable creatures will be captured on film.

Ocean creatures

Much of the world's marine life remains a mystery. New species of large sea creatures, including beaked whales, are still being discovered. Future explorers may find that creatures thought to be legendary, such as the Giant Sea Serpent, really exist.

FUTURE EXPLORATION

Today, we can see satellite photographs of almost anywhere on Earth via the Internet. It may seem that there is nowhere left to explore, but in reality, there is a lot left to discover – in the oceans, in the rainforests, and under Antarctica's ice sheets. This is also the start of a new era of Space exploration, with plans to return to the Moon and to travel to other planets.

GLOSSARY

Aborigines
The name given by British settlers to the native people of Australia. It means "original inhabitants" in Latin.

African Association
A club set up in 1788 by a group of wealthy Britons to organize the exploration of Africa.

Amber
The fossilized resin of ancient trees. It has been highly prized since ancient times for use in jewellery.

Antarctic
The cold southernmost region of Earth, surrounding the South Pole.

Apollo Programme
A US Space programme that ran from 1966 to 1975, and sent 12 astronauts to the Moon.

Arctic
The cold northernmost region of Earth, surrounding the North Pole.

Asteroid
An object orbiting the Sun, usually between Mars and Jupiter, in a region called the asteroid belt. Asteroids are made of rock or metal.

Astrolabe
An instrument for measuring latitude from the height of the midday Sun.

Astronaut
The US term for a crew member of a spacecraft. It derives from two Greek words, *astron* (star) and *nautes* (sailor).

Aztecs
A warlike Mexican people, whose empire lasted from the early 14th century until 1521, when they were conquered by the Spanish.

Barometer
An instrument for measuring air pressure – the weight of the invisible gases in Earth's atmosphere. Early barometers used a column of mercury in a tube, which rose or fell according to air pressure.

Bathyscaphe
A craft for deep-sea diving, invented in the 1940s by August Piccard. Unlike a bathysphere, it is self-propelled and not connected to a surface vessel. Its name in Greek means "ship of the deep".

Bathysphere
A spherical craft for deep-sea diving. It is not powered, but is lowered into the sea from a surface vessel.

Blue Nile
The Blue Nile is the shorter of two rivers that join together to form the Nile, the longest river on Earth. It flows from Lake Tana in Ethiopia to Khartoum in Sudan, where it joins the White Nile.

Botanist
A scientist who specializes in the study of plants.

Cape
A point or head of land, sticking out into the sea.

Caravan
A company of travellers journeying together for safety.

Caravel
A Portuguese ship with lateen (triangular) sails, used for voyages of exploration in the 15th century.

Carrack
A large European trading ship, with square sails. Carracks were used from the 15th to the 16th centuries.

Comet
An object made from ice, dust, and rocky particles, orbiting the Sun.

Conquistador
The Spanish word for a conqueror, specifically referring to the 16th-century Spanish conquerors of the native peoples of Central and South America.

Cosmonaut
The Russian term for a crew member of a spacecraft. It derives from two Greek words, *kosmos* (universe) and *nautes* (sailor).

Cryobot
A robot-controlled probe, designed to penetrate ice sheets. It has a heated tip for melting the ice.

Dead reckoning
A way of working out a ship's position by recording its speed and direction, and marking the course travelled on a chart.

Dreamtime
The Australian aboriginal name for the time of the creation of the world by spirit beings.

Empire
A large area, including different peoples, ruled by a single state. There have been many empires throughout history, usually created by military conquest.

European Space Agency
A European organization established in 1975, to carry out Space exploration. It currently has 18 member nations.

Evolution
The process of gradual development of species over time.

Exploration
The search for unknown lands or places, or new routes to known lands.

Friar
A member of a Roman Catholic religious brotherhood. A friar's main role was to preach, but they also served as teachers and ambassadors for medieval European rulers.

Frostbite
This condition occurs when human body tissues freeze in cold temperatures. The most vulnerable areas are the ears, nose, cheeks, fingers, and toes. It can lead to amputation of the affected part.

Gemini Programme
A US Space programme that ran from 1964 to 1966, which prepared the way for Moon missions.

Geography
The study of Earth's surface. The name in Greek means "writing about Earth".

Geology
The study of Earth's crust. Geologists study how rocks, oil, and gas form.

Hubble Space Telescope
A Space telescope launched in 1990, which orbits Earth. It is named after the US astronomer, Edwin Hubble. Outside Earth's atmosphere, it can see further and more clearly than telescopes on the ground.

Hydrothermal vent
A crack in the ocean floor, where hot gases flow up from Earth's crust, heating the surrounding water.

Incas
The native people of Peru, who ruled a great empire from the 1430s until the 16th century, when they were conquered by the Spanish.

Incense
A substance from the gum and resin of certain trees, which produces sweet-smelling smoke when burned.

International Space Station
A Space laboratory that orbits Earth. Its first part was launched by the Russians in 1998. It is a joint project of the USA, Russia, Japan, Canada, and the European Union.

Inuit
The native people of the Canadian Arctic and Greenland. The name comes from the Inuit language, and simply means "human beings".

Junk
A Chinese ocean-going ship with a flat bottom, and sails that are often square and stiffened with bamboo.

Khan
The title of a ruler in Mongolian and in other central Asian languages.

Lateen
A triangular sail.

Latitude
A position to the north or south of the equator, which is an imaginary line around the middle of Earth.

I'm lost for words

I've broken down

I can't see the point

That's enough of your latitude

Words are all I have...

Longitude
A position to the east or west of a given point. Today, we measure longitude from a line running through Greenwich, England.

Manioc
A plant grown in the tropics, whose starchy roots are eaten as food.

Maroon
To leave someone behind during a sea voyage on an island or coast.

Mercury Programme
The first US manned spaceflight programme, which ran from 1959 to 1963.

Mid-Atlantic Ridge
An undersea mountain range which runs down the centre of the Atlantic Ocean, from the Arctic to the Antarctic.

Ming
A Chinese dynasty, or family of rulers. The Ming dynasty ruled China from 1368 to 1644.

Mongols
A warlike people from Mongolia that conquered a huge empire in Asia in the 13th century.

Monsoon
A wind that swaps direction in different seasons.

Mutiny
A rebellion against someone in authority, particularly by sailors against their captain.

NASA
The National Aeronautics and Space Administration, which was set up in 1958 by the US government to run their Space exploration programme.

Naturalist
A scientist who studies animals and plants.

Natural selection
The means by which new living species are created, according to Charles Darwin's theory of evolution. Within a species, certain individuals are born with features that help them survive to have offspring. The features passed on are said to be "selected by nature". Small changes build up over time, and new species appear.

Navigation
The science of finding a way from one place to another.

Navigational instrument
A device, such as a magnetic compass or an astrolabe, used in navigation.

Northeast passage
A sea route from Europe over the top of Russia to the Pacific Ocean and Asia.

Northwest passage
A sea route from Europe over the top of North America to the Pacific Ocean and Asia.

Oceanography
The science of the oceans. This includes the study of marine life, currents, waves, weather, and the movements of Earth's crust.

Phoenicians
An ancient seafaring and trading people, whose homeland was on the coast of modern-day Lebanon.

Pilot
A skilled navigator.

Plateau
An area of high flat land.

Poles
The points at the top and bottom of Earth, around which it revolves.

Prester John
A legendary Christian king, thought to live somewhere in Africa or Asia during the Middle Ages. He was said to be immensely rich and powerful.

Saga
A long story written for entertainment in the Middle Ages. Icelandic sagas are our main source of evidence of Viking exploration.

Sargasso Sea
A seaweed-covered area in the middle of the Atlantic Ocean.

Satellite
An artificial object orbiting Earth or another planetary body.

Scurvy
A disease caused by a lack of vitamin C, once common on long expeditions when fresh food ran out.

Seismic exploration
A method of exploring underground, using artificially created shock waves. Seismic exploration is used to search for gas and oil deposits.

Sherpas
The native people of the southern side of the Himalayan Mountains, in Nepal and India. Sherpas are excellent climbers and mountain guides.

Silk Road
A collection of trade routes from China to the Mediterranean. Many merchants travelled along it to buy silk from China.

Skraelings
The name given by Vikings to the native Americans they encountered. It is thought to come from their word *skra* (skin). Unlike the Vikings, who wore clothes of woven wool, Skraelings dressed in animal skins.

Snowmobile
A vehicle for travelling over snow and ice. It is propelled by tracks at the rear, and steered by skis at the front.

Sonar
The use of sound waves to locate objects by the echoes they send back. Ships and submarines use sonar to detect underwater objects.

Space probe
An unmanned spacecraft sent into Space to study other planets and moons.

Spices
The seeds, leaves, or bark of plants used to flavour food.

Sputnik
The name given to a series of robotic spacecraft, which were launched into orbit by the USSR between 1957 and 1962. Sputnik 1 was the first satellite. Sputnik 2 carried a dog called Laika.

Strait
A narrow passage of water joining two large areas of water.

Terra Australis Incognita
The name given to a continent, once wrongly believed to exist in the southern hemisphere. The name means "Unknown Southern land".

Thule
A northern land – probably Iceland or Norway – visited by the Ancient Greek explorer Pytheas.

USSR
The Union of Soviet Socialist Republics (or Soviet Union) was a Eurasian state, dominated by Russia. It existed from 1922 until it fell apart in 1991.

Vikings
The seafaring people of Scandinavia, who lived between the 8th and 11th centuries.

Vostok Programme
A USSR Space programme that ran from 1961, and sent the first man and woman into Space.

Wallace Line
A boundary dividing the animals and plants of East and West Malaya. It is named after the Victorian naturalist, Alfred Russell Wallace.

White Nile
The White Nile is the longer of the two rivers that join together to form the Nile River.

I'm going to bone up on my definitions

I shouldn't fly over this bit

Sonar, yet so far

Arr, who be the captain of this ship?

I've clouded my view

INDEX

It's magical!

It's time to travel some more

Howard's away

Acknowledgements

Dorling Kindersley
would like to thank
Caitlin Doyle for
proof-reading, Jackie
Brind for the index,
Megan Lucas for
editorial assistance,
and Millie Popovic
for design assistance.

Some Brainwaves were
injured in the making of
this book, but they are
now fully recovered.